NURTURING MASCULINITIES

NURTURING MASCULINITIES

Men, Food, and Family in Contemporary Egypt

NEFISSA NAGUIB

UNIVERSITY OF TEXAS PRESS ◆ *Austin*

All photographs in the book were taken by the author.

Requests for permission to reproduce material from this work
should be sent to:
   Permissions
   University of Texas Press
   P.O. Box 7819
   Austin, TX 78713-7819
   http://utpress.utexas.edu/index.php/rp-form

♾ The paper used in this book meets the minimum requirements of
ANSI/NISO Z39.48-1992 (R1997) (Permanence of Paper).

LIBRARY OF CONGRESS CATALOGING-IN-PUBLICATION DATA

Naguib, Nefissa, 1960– author.
   Nurturing masculinities : men, food, and family in contemporary
Egypt / Nefissa Naguib. — First edition, 2015.
      pages   cm
   Includes bibliographical references and index.
      ISBN 978-1-4773-0553-9 (cloth : alk. paper) — ISBN 978-1-4773-0710-6
(pbk. : alk. paper) — ISBN 978-1-4773-0554-6 (library e-book) —
ISBN 978-1-4773-0555-3 (nonlibrary e-book)
      1. Food habits—Egypt. 2. Masculinity—Egypt. 3. Sex role—
Egypt. 4. Egyptians—Food. 5. Food—Social aspects—Egypt.
I. Title.
   GT2853.E.3N34   2015
   394.1′20962—dc23   2015001625

doi:10.7560/ 305539

THIS BOOK IS DEDICATED TO MY FATHER.

CONTENTS

PREFACE AND ACKNOWLEDGMENTS

WE ALL HAVE PERSONAL MEMORIES of meals—memories evoked by a fragrance, a taste, the season, colors, a close relative, a friend, a passing mood, or a certain place. And almost everybody has a story or two about a meal with a loved one. One of the fondest memories I have is of sharing watermelon slices and feta cheese with my dear father in the summer on our balcony in Cairo. He was particularly fond of accompanying this snack with a glass of cold beer, from which I was occasionally allowed to sip the foam. Seeing my mother as she prepared and offered snacks—and other, more complicated meals—with such love and commitment instilled in me enduring culinary curiosity. I have them both to thank for this book.

My decades of fieldwork in Cairo were enriched by the friendship and good-humored assistance of my interlocutors. Without them there would be no stories to tell. They opened their hearts and homes to me; no words can capture their hospitality and trust in me.

Two lovely women gave so much of themselves and their wisdom to this book. A decade or so ago, and in between projects on global moments and the messy outcomes of war on human lives, I had a long conversation with my dearest friend, Beth Baron, that stayed with me. This book contains none of the plans we made, but it has made me revisit the question of caring and our next adventures together. When my very dear friend Marcia Inhorn told me, "You simply have to write that book," it was the beginning of a longlasting friendship that I value deeply. She was with me every step of the way. Thank you.

Warm thanks to my dear Bonnie Rose Schulman for copyediting this manuscript in its different stages. She commented and made suggestions with such kindness and sweetness.

I have benefited greatly from stimulating discussions about foodways and ways of tracing human life and food with Randi Håland. I would like to thank Christine Amadou, Nancy Frank, Ingvild Flaskerud, Catharina Raudvere, Annika Rabo, Susanne Dahlgren, Kjersti Larsen, Carol Counihan, David Sutton, Suad Joseph, Laila Prager, Johannes Becker, Jennifer Olmsted, and Mustafa Riad for listening to me or reading parts of this manuscript at different points and giving me encouragement.

The Research Council of Norway gave me the greatest gift a researcher could get: the time to do fieldwork and write. I wrote several chapters of this book during my stay as visiting scholar at the Institut d'études de l'Islam et des Sociétés du Monde Musulman (IISMM) in Paris during the spring of 2012; I would like to express my gratitude to Bernard Heyberger for inviting me and showing interest in my work. Thanks also to Nathalie Bernard-Maugiron, Rémy Madiner, and Hélène Dauchez for making my stay at the institute so agreeable. I am grateful also for the critical institutional support from the Chr. Michelsen Institute.

I am immensely indebted to my editor, Jim Burr, for telling me to write a book my grandmother could read. He insightfully and gently engaged with this manuscript. I want to thank both reviewers for their close reading and invaluable feedback, comments, questions, and criticisms. It is truly a privilege to have one's work read so thoroughly.

This book is about the ways we give, share, and cherish the love and care of family. For me there is no better way of doing that than enjoying food at the table. This book would not have been possible without the smitten enthusiasm of my husband, Bjørn, who always makes sure I go on my culinary journeys and who made sure that I was well nourished while writing this book. Our three daughters, Nora, Maria, and Anissa, and our son-in-law, Andreas, all contributed in their own very loving and sweet ways to this book.

NURTURING MASCULINITIES

INTRODUCTION

There is one idea that stands out about Egyptian men and food. Contentment is the feeling a man should have after his meal. In all conversations, men talked about this particular desire for fulfilling and satisfying food.

FIELDWORK NOTES, CAIRO, JUNE 2012

I FIRST GOT SMILES, even laughs, from men in Cairo. Some considered food an odd topic of interest for a *doctora* (scholar): "Are you going to write a cookbook or write about us like some bizarre tribe?" they asked laughingly. Nonetheless, they did talk to me about food: they shared their favorite recipes and critiqued my choice of ingredients; they demonstrated how to tap a watermelon and listen carefully for the sound of ripeness; they taught me that small pieces of bread must be folded into the shape of a cat's ear and that everything tastes better when cooked with *samna baladi* (clarified butter).

I heard about favorite dishes; food politics and activism; their mothers' stews; childhood memories; and stories of love, food, and marriage. They told me that meals are not meals if they are not shared with conviviality and lightheartedness. In detail, they spoke about food justice, the religious duty to share food, their wives' cooking skills, the tastes of rice, and the scent of passing by the local bakery on the way home. They talked about their attempts to teach their children polite and authentic Egyptian meal etiquette and to give them sweet childhood memories of family meals.

As the years passed and my fieldwork progressed, I observed and listened to men as they planned meals and then shopped for, ate, enjoyed, and worried about food. Fear and anger about food prices were often followed by smiles and jokes about the appetites of Egyptian men. Farouk Mansour, a café owner whom I have known for close to three decades, presented a prevailing indictment of the present mode of being an Egyptian "ordinary man," as he put it. He said, "We never had as many fatal diseases like today. Groceries did not have as much food as today, but what they had was fresh, tasty, and affordable. We did not die from heart attacks because of worry about our way of eating or how we were going to feed our family."

Farouk's criticism of "today" is consistent with my other interlocutors' views of their lives "before" and "today." Feeding and eating are core components of the deterioration of everything from physical well-being to emotional fulfillment. But then Farouk turned back to me and added:

> The Egyptian man is kindhearted and responsible. Even if life is more stressful today than before, men like us find a way with craftiness and wit. . . . Also, if you have enough, you can buy anything. Today we have supermarkets full of food. You can buy whatever you are in the mood for. Nothing makes men happier than to see the smiles on the children's faces when they see their favorite meal. It's worth the whole world.

In Farouk's view, as in many narratives I heard during my work in Egypt, there is an odd and ambivalent meshing of memory making, longings for past forms of family life, striving to accommodate obligations, and enthusiasm for modernity and contemporary life. Unsurprisingly, beneath the surface similarities of "men like us" were individual variations, which are explored throughout the book. Uncanny associations with traditions and modernity, along with contrasting meanings and coherences between men's social values and food practices, give room for reflection, especially when the scope of men's domesticities is broadened and deepened into the idea of nurturing masculinities.

My concept of "nurturing masculinities" has been developed through exploring men's relation to food, and it builds on the growing body of literature on "lived masculinities" (Inhorn 2012), which unsettles the dominant trope of relying on domination and patriarchy when discussing Middle Eastern men.

The book tells the stories of ordinary Egyptian men and the cultural roots that connect them with food and domestic life. These are stories of men who care deeply about their families. We hear them speak about extraordinary economic hardship, politics, and activism; we feel them standing in endless breadlines under a scorching sun; we hear them recollect the taste, feel, and fragrance of food; and we feel their desires to feed their families well and often.

These accounts tell of the memories and aspirations of male interlocutors who lived and moved around in Cairo's lower-class and lower-middle-class neighborhoods. Each chapter centers on men's experiences as told to me in numerous interviews and conversations, but also during spontaneous moments of grocery shopping, cooking, and eating.

Nurturing Masculinities is full of fragments of history, nostalgia, faith, aspiration, and appetite. Alongside these positive reflections, however, are tensions between personal desires and the men's quality of life—when the determination to be a dependable man is painful and the contemporary world doesn't always make perfect sense. There are several things going on in the men's food stories, resulting in the closely woven coherence of these thick ethnographic descriptions. I hope the stories about taste, smell, texture, and their combinations, as reflected in daily consumption, illuminate something about men's concerns and the ambivalent embrace of contemporary social life in Cairo.

A LITTLE BACKGROUND

Cairo is friendly, noisy, dirty, smelly, polluted, and intensely crowded. Since the 1970s, the city has experienced tremendous growth and change in its urban sprawl. New, gated communities that cater to the affluent middle classes form a ring road along pockets of informal communities that house millions of people.

In Arabic, *Masr* means "Egypt"; for Cairenes, *Masr* also means "Cairo." The central point of Greater Cairo is Midan al-Tahrir (Tahrir Square)—the epicenter of the 2011 Egyptian revolution. When it was constructed in 1860, based on a model of Paris's Place de l'Étoile, the Egyptian army and the Ministry of Defense were located in the neighborhood (J. Abu-Lughod 1971).

To the east, Tahrir Square leads to older Cairo; its many bridges across the Nile link the central city to newer districts. In *The Book of Jewish Food*, Claudia Roden (1999, 4) offers a fitting description of Cairo as a city that is divided into "two cities that turned their backs on each other."

> One looked like Paris, because Khedive Ismail . . . had
> wanted to pull Egypt into Europe and brought in European
> architects to build it. The other had narrow meandering
> streets, mausoleums, and public baths; fountains with curvy
> iron grilles and windows screened by wooden lattices; Coptic
> churches and mosques with minarets rising into the sky like
> delicately embroidered candles.

Roden's observations recall the city's most penetrating cosmopolitan moment, sometime between the 1850s and 1950s. These years marked the end of one imperial period—the Ottoman—and the continuation of another—the British. The city has since undergone many social, political, and economic transformations. Yet city markers from its cosmopolitan past endure, and traces of what once existed remain. Contemporary Cairo is still divided by aesthetic contrasts,

FIGURE 1. Bird's-eye view of Cairo, 2001.

shifting colors, moods, and spirits that linger in the memory of the city's past. Often, especially in people's stories, Cairo is remembered by associating social traditions from the past with recollections of the taste, smell, texture, and price of food.

Besides trying to capture the tone, fabric, and odors of Cairo, this book provides an account of men whose lives have been shaped by the texture and flavors of the city, and divided by historical durations and rhythms. The chapters look at the ways in which men remember past events, respond to day-to-day demands, and find a balance between struggling and thriving as men doing what men do.

Each of the stories is about the complexities of change, lived experiences, and the valuation of food. Alongside men's food stories are memories of moments that reveal themselves through concrete practices and their own sweet and melancholy narratives and modes of transmission. According to Sidney Mintz, "Eating is never a 'purely biological' activity," but rather one of many arenas in which people invest "a basic activity with social meaning(s)" that are both "symbolic" and "communicated symbolically" and that "also have histories" (1996, 7). I propose that food memories are also about cultural repetitions and processes. Food reflects, in part, the interdependence between men and their memories, attachments, and significant relationships. To talk about men and food, then, is to reflect on the extent to which men's domesticity is embedded in the wider historical and cultural milieus from which men's accounts emerge.

WHEN I BEGAN FIELDWORK in Cairo on men and family life, I gained insight into men's personal experiences through a set of interviews conducted on another topic—histories of food. I seemed to obtain more reflective, friendlier, and more personal accounts of men's lives when conversations turned to shopping for, providing, and cooking food. We traced the paths of many meals during interviews supposedly focused on Egyptian manhood and family relationships.

Cairo is a city where food and its circulation are crucial to a sense of identity, family, and public interaction: bread being baked or carried around on wooden grills; cries from vegetable peddlers; the smoky fragrance of roasting sweet potatoes or corn grilled on charcoal and sold from wooden carts; the occasional stall of wooden cages crowded with live chickens, ducks, rabbits, and pigeons, along with eggs carefully arranged on straw in baskets; butchers trimming cuts from lamb, camel, or beef carcasses hanging on hooks or resting on wooden blocks—these are some of the visible foodways that constitute daily life in the streets and alleys of Cairo.

Activities like choosing favorite restaurants, bakeries, pastry shops, cafés, and takeout venues; ordering food for delivery from the neighborhood supermarket or butcher; and picking up the weekly groceries at a mall all shape daily food activities for the middle class. For the poorer majority of the population, meals are shaped by the availability of particular foods, the areas where grocery shopping is done, the allowances of ration cards, the length of breadlines, and preferences about which food stalls offer the tastiest and cheapest

FIGURE 2. Butcher in Old Cairo, 2011.

breakfasts. There is a food stall on nearly every street corner in Cairo. Every morning, men of all classes gather around the same ones. There is the smell of sizzling garlic, onions, falafel, fava beans (*ful*), and hot peppers. Vendors' swift hands open rounds of bread and fill them with each man's favorite meal. The ambience is convivial and informal. Conversations hum between the man serving breakfast and the men eating their food. One of my interlocutors introduced me to his "sandwich man and breakfast chums" by saying that I was "writing a book about Egyptian men." They nodded and invited me to join them for breakfast. "You have come to the right place," the food seller said while he prepared his special plate of *ful* "for the lady." He moved to the side of his mobile stall and offered me a plate of warm puréed fava beans simmering in olive oil and lemon, with one hard-boiled egg floating in the middle, served with warm bread. "With *ful* and bread we are all the same," said one of the breakfasting men before saying good-bye and walking off to catch his bus to work.

MEN AND FOOD

Food provides an extraordinary means of investigation because it resonates with attitudes and emotions related to men's and women's understanding of the self and others and of their underlying interactions. A meal is a gift that sates desire, gives pleasure, evokes memories, and creates attachments. The accounts in this book rest on Egyptian men's voices, on how they convey food's extraordinary ability to historicize, encode, and regulate their relationships with their spouses and children.

This book explores the role of food in forming Egyptian men's identities and shaping their practices in daily life. Case studies examine food as a medium of social relations, as a tool for constructing notions of masculinity, and as a way to reveal perceptions of class, generation, gender, and other features of men's identities.

Nurturing Masculinities looks to the notion of culture and food as an "art of living" and as a way for men to be in the world. My premise is that it is possible to identify, within a particular community, significant sets of foodways that constitute systems and provide overlapping messages about people, their attachments, and aspects of their cultures and lives. By operating on different levels, these messages present variations and contradictions about life as lived within the rich scope of practice, local living, and global developments.

Fieldwork for this book involved three winters and one summer from 2011 to 2013; interviews in Arabic were conducted with men I knew from previous studies in Egypt in the 1980s and again in the years 2005–2008. I interviewed fifty men between 2011 and 2013 specifically for this book, selecting the most relevant stories for inclusion. The picture that emerges is not homogeneous. Descriptions and analyses of the everyday reveal that although ordinary people carry out similar activities, they live their lives in different ways.

Although I present these stories as authentically as possible, I ground them in theory. Some were audiotaped, and some were taken from field notes. The stories are not composed of structured plots, with a beginning, a middle, and an end. They were not told in one day, but over a long period of time. Although my goal is to bring out the resonance of these voices, I also "construct" the outcome.

The oral-history fieldwork for this project was easy and pleasant. Men wanted to talk about food preferences, food memories, buying groceries, breadlines, feeding their families, and their food outreach activities. Each chapter studies how aspects of men's identities and everyday involvements are created and then parlayed into wider networks of meaning and value. Men discuss how uncertainty about food and the power of food lead to deep questions about what it means to be an Egyptian man.

All the interview subjects are from Cairo and are between thirty and seventy years old. Some are ordinary family men with no political affiliation; others, often younger, are at least somewhat involved with the Society of the Muslim Brothers (the Muslim Brotherhood). Regardless, when asked to define themselves, they always included the phrase "*ibn al-balad*," which literally means "son of the country," in contrast to "*ibn al-nas*," or "son of the people," which implies coming from elsewhere and having no roots in the country.[1] My interlocutors were all Muslim middle-class and lower-middle-class men with ties to popular inner-city quarters located on either side of Tahrir Square—medieval Cairo to the south, and the neighborhoods of Bulaq Abu 'Ala, Shubra, Fagala, and Abassia to the north and northeast. Hence, although these are lower-income areas, they are not strictly tied to economic class or consumption. Several of my interlocutors with middle-class incomes continued to live in

1. Sawsan el-Messiri (1978, 4) explains how the phrase reveals characteristic nuances that can be understood only within the specific context where it is used. "*Ibn al-balad*" would imply a Cairene, since Cairo and Egypt have always been identified in Egyptian consciousness with the same name, "*Masr.*"

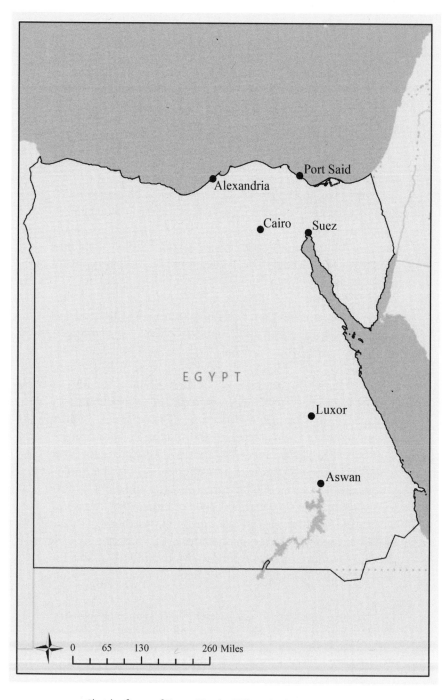

MAP 1. Sketch of map of Egypt. Map by William Soohoo; *sources*: Esri, HERE, DeLorme, MapMyIndia, © OpenSteetMap contributors and the GIS community.

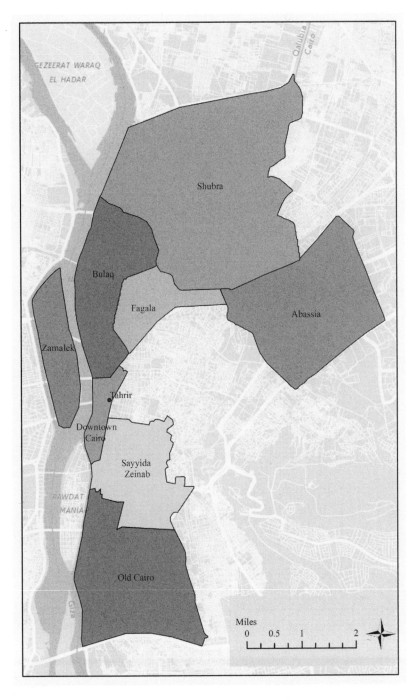

GEZEERAT WARAQ
EL HADAR

Qalubia
Cairo

Shubra

Bulaq

Fagala

Abassia

Zamalek

Tahrir

Downtown
Cairo

Sayyida
Zeinab

RAWDAT
MANIA

Old Cairo

Giza

Miles

0   0.5   1   2

MAP 2. Rough sketch of field sites. Map by William Soohoo; *sources*: Esri,
HERE, DeLorme, MapMyIndia, © OpenSteetMap contributors and the GIS
community.

FIGURE 3. Father and daughter in Tahrir Square, 2012, one year after the ousting of President Hosni Mubarak.

their childhood neighborhoods, while others moved to more upscale neighborhoods. The important point is that my interlocutors had roots in these areas and continued to speak about themselves as *awlad al-balad* (plural of *ibn al-balad*).

The men in this book felt strongly about the things they eat and how and with whom they eat them. I use life histories to bring this forward. My reason for doing so connects with Marcia Inhorn's (2012, 17) proposition that stories should be used to validate ethnographies. The stories, conversations, and observations included here are condensed, simplified, and edited in order to provide a clear narrative and elucidate its role as an instrument of basic inquiry about "being in the world." Moreover, the use of narrative can evolve into a conversation about empirically controversial and difficult areas, such as the place of culture and the significance of historicity in an analysis like this one. This type of exposition is necessary in order to understand the basis of my claim that these stories can be generalized and used to interpret the wider universe of men's worlds.

Stories in this book link the sentimental and the intellectual, the experiential (what some men know about the world) and the aspirational (what they hope to achieve for themselves and their loved ones). Food has the mental and physical potency to both create and destroy human integrity and attachment. My premise is that food—along with memories of preparing and eating meals—offers a sense of what it means to have a life.

This book returns to the promise of anthropology as an exploration of human social and political potentialities. For me, the essence of anthropology is its ability to address the social and political imaginaries of human beings, especially those likely to be intense and widespread. So it is among the men in this account, who worry and muse about the state of food affairs. They are able to theorize their own lives, speaking about the general social consciousness of radical shifts in the circumstances and the shaping of life projects.

This attempt at reorientation examines (new) social imaginings and their formation at the juncture of everyday uncertainties in Egypt. Providing, preparing, and eating food involves an immediacy of experience that allows anthropology to interpret how people reexamine their social and political forms of possibility. My objective is to bring out the pasts, presents, and futures (and the forces that inhibit them) of bread and other foods, as discussed and imagined by men. Consequently, writing about food and men addresses the processes by which meaning and life stylization are constructed. This is one way that anthropology can, I believe, evaluate the nature of human direction and potentiality during uncertain times.

It is difficult to envisage and theorize how human agency is linked with human subjectivity, with forms of the possible, and with new ways of conceiving the human subject and its relations to the world. How do we encompass human life and pursuit? How do we account for people's projects of being in the world, including their desires to transform—at times, radically—the conditions that make them? The men's stories recounted here are combined with broader reflections on issues to which those narratives relate.

FOOD AND GENDER STORIES

Stories can be biographies, autobiographies, ethnohistories, oral histories, life histories, life stories, living histories, and narratives. Stories, like recorded histories, have an internal logic. In a sense, stories illustrate people's reflexive engagements with their own lives. For those who recount the stories of other people, it is important not to confuse history with story. This point is of particular importance when dealing with life histories, in which history and ethnography can mingle and interact. These stories have a way of moving beyond the recorded and depending largely on reminiscences and feelings present at the time of their telling. Stories constitute incomplete evidence. They are human dramas about what people remember, want to remember, or cannot forget.

Then there is my retelling of stories. I have shaped these narratives by selecting only certain bits and pieces of them. Thus, my interlocutors and I are both creating and perhaps even inventing traditions. We might agree with Peter Gottschalk (2000, 7), who writes that narratives' main trait of significance is that "those who communicate them believe that the stories depict actual events of their past." The stories concern not what is true or false in an ethnographic sense, but how the content of narratives create real lives for those telling their stories. In previous work, I have argued that life stories are about the past, whether near or distant, and must be told as part of both the ethnographic present and "the felt force of past events" (Sutton 2001, 1). Retrospectively, I think life stories are more complicated. Noting what this link between past and present excludes in human relationships is as crucial as recording what it includes.

This is a story about how food is an endlessly evolving enactment of men's and women's interactions, family life, commensality, and social mobilization. Literature on food and gender dynamics suggests that gender does not differ from other social allocations, such as race, generation, class, and ethnicity. Gender acknowledges and addresses differences, but gender, like ethnicity, can be imagined; so too can associated differences between men, women, and food (Counihan 1999).

Moreover, feminist scholars have been especially innovative in analyzing the relations between food and subjectivity, exploring how food systems give material form to social identities, inequalities, and power relations and naturalize them in daily, embodied experiences (see Counihan 1999).

Cooking has been claimed as a key source of women's power (Kahn 1986; Jansen 1997; Counihan 1999; Weismantel 1988). However, in some ways, men retain the primary control over food (Khouri-Dagher 1996; Sutton 2001). The literature on masculinities in anthropology is astonishingly silent on food from the perspectives of Arab men. In the analysis of men and food in Egypt, patriarchy looms much larger than do foodways.

The anthropology of food and gender has emerged in response to particular cultural, socioeconomic, and political changes (Delaney 1991; Counihan and Kaplan 1998; Jansen 1997; Khan 1986; Mintz and Du Bois 2002; Weismantel 1988). As a consequence of expanding research into women's and men's personal and social lives, food appears both as an influence and as a specific kind of delineator of social order or social boundaries (see, for example, Douglas 1966; Lévi-Strauss 1966; Sutton 2001; Wilk 1999). In the contemporary world, debates about food and gender are often debates about empowerment, households, and negotiations. Food has become a particular aspect of the politics of gender. Elements of food in different communities seem to be sought as criteria of men's and women's cultural uniqueness and originality.

Sidney Mintz and Christine Du Bois (2002) point out that gender and food resemble other social allocations that define human identities and belongings. This similarity may explain the growing interest in food as an aspect of reconstructing personal and collective lives. It is thus not surprising that human struggle and the creation of new social movements draw on food as part of the transformation of societal relationships, cultural practices, and men's and women's roles.

But even as food creates new connections and new roles, it does not necessarily obliterate old links and habits. To remember the past, we need to recognize and understand relationships and to know how to share these references. Stories are memories of the past that merge with current life. But using narratives historically is awkward, because they are just that—stories. They are conversations, statements, and remarks, sometimes carelessly conveyed. But the use of stories communicates social acts; it lends spirit and vitality to significant testimonies about why people do what they do.

Paul Ricoeur's insights help contemporary scholars in their approaches to narratives. He explains that narratives are fundamental as instructions in human experiences through time. Ricoeur's (1984) work on narratives is the theoretical backdrop for Peter Gottschalk's work. Gottschalk (2000, 70) goes beyond Ricoeur, recognizing the "reflective tool of history that connects lived time with cosmic time: place." Narratives exist in context, and should be seen in relation to time and space: "Narratives regarding the past offer a particularly useful tool of examination because by their very nature they often include important ingredients for identity: references to the present community in time and space" (69). Indeed, we can interpret narratives best when observing their tellers' social interactions and relations.

My interlocutors regularly began their accounts by recalling, for example, childhood meals or the price of specific food items: "At home we used to eat . . ." or "I remember when watermelons cost . . ." At the source of recollection lies the ability to retrieve a story. "Life consists of retellings," writes Edward M. Bruner (1986); it is a reminder of the story's lifeline and of how it is told. Narratives of meals or food costs belong to memories that are culturally shaped by the places they occupy in people's lives; they lend themselves to our understanding of how men and women re-create their "sites" of memory (Nora 1996), which are taken up in their telling. Knowing history through narrative implies that men's stories are more than just remembrances from other times. Their accounts combine experiences with nostalgia, adding to the poetic, emotional load that food is made, retrospectively, to carry. In this book, men often link grocery shopping, food outreach, and family meals with caring, giving, marriage, and parenting; financial concerns (familial and global), political rage, and social pressure; and accomplishment and satisfaction. The stories show how, cumulatively and over time, small, everyday events surrounding food have broader implications for being an Egyptian man.

Men's food struggles reverberate through their everyday lives: their economic and political battles, their intimate relations, and their defense of culture, traditions, and religion. This book rests on men's voices, on how they convey food's extraordinary ability to historicize, encode, and regulate their relationships. Alongside food, other themes about events and activities emerge—locally and sometimes globally.

THE MALE PORTION

By bringing together the food concerns of Egyptian men of different classes, politics, and ages—and their struggles to feed their families during uncertain times—this book provides a new density and definition to the complex negotiations of gender and other social allocations that underpin social and cultural continuities. These men help us understand how contemporary redefinitions of Egyptian domesticity, gender roles, concepts such as "husband" and "father," proper images of men, and the relations between faith and popular customs are powerfully shaped by everyday food practices.

In addition, this book is concerned with the image of masculinity as a product of time. History, politics, and economics bring with them new voices that contest the monopoly of power, hierarchy, and gender images. Food provisioning entails a sense of vulnerability that pervades social life. For example, Fahmi Hassan, an enthusiastic farmer turned gardener and florist described in chapter 1, likes to talk about the divine distribution of life: "Every man is given a portion in life." For him, food is not just something he uses to feed his family or, in his words, to "fill their stomachs"; rather, providing it is a mark of proper male behavior and day-to-day morality.

One must examine the particularities of individual lives in order to understand what at the outset may seem quite ordinary. Sarah Pink (2012) notes that everyday goings-on are a challenge for the person trying to analyze them. She quotes Michael Gardiner (2000, 385): "We cannot simply 'go on' the everyday; we are 'always already' immersed in it." I agree with Pink's (2012, 31) conclusion that to use the everyday "requires the recognition that researchers are in the same way always part of the lives and worlds they are researching." As a life-giving substance, food has immediate implications for the everyday, a phenomenon whose intensity warrants additional consideration.

Indeed, the key question, here as elsewhere, is not why everyday food practices should matter (they must), but how they are pathway systems that produce relations between persons and between people and the world. Because this book is concerned with men's stories as memic reflections of relationships and practices (Harrison 2006), I find that Fredrik Barth's way of knowing might provide an analytical language for interrogating other people's everyday. To come to grips with the Balinese everyday, Barth did not question their world; instead, he observed "the process by which people endow their life with meaning" (Barth 1993, 95). While values and institutions make up the structure under which men and women live, they do not explain how people act in their everyday lives.

To understand—to come to grips with men's everyday happiness, concerns, and sorrows—we must better understand

FIGURE 4. Bread for the family, 1998.

intentions and actions. But this requires understanding how everyday life takes place. Barth (1993, 160) writes that this is possible "with a reasonable amount of patience and genuine interest in the lives of particular individuals we encounter." Expanding on this notion, I suggest that understanding everyday goings, comings, and conversations depends on taking to heart what the men in the book do and say, and on regarding their reflections as displays of culture or patriarchal variation.

The men in this book lived (and continue to live) in the midst of change, and the complexities of flux affect their relations with their spouses and children. Men in contemporary Egypt do not repeat established repertoires in order to connect with their world; they mold and reproduce relationships and practices at a time of great uncertainty, with serious consequences for their lives.

Barth (1994, 355) asks us to study closely the reality that people choose to mold and produce in their attempts to give meaning to the world, "in conformity with an embracing construct of balance and harmony between cosmos, society and morally excellent souls." In writing about the experiences of individuals, Barth uses everyday experiences to reveal how knowledge is always in flux. Hence, we are advised to appropriate "knowledge" rather than "culture." Knowledge can then provide theoretical avenues for talking about knowing and being in the world.

But a knowledge system is a conceptual approach largely concerned with constructing a coherent sénse of self with little regard for narratives or forms of temporality. *Nurturing Masculinities* calls for a return to culture in the sense of what in an earlier work I explored as "formulating grammars" (Naguib 2009). My enterprise is a thick description of a time when men responded to and carried forward ideas and practices about food. The anthropology of Marshall Sahlins remains, in my view, one of the most pertinent assessments of the significance of culture. Sahlins uses culture to argue for the uses of history. He writes that culture is flexible when personal histories are being addressed, especially within the framework of people situating their lives and defining themselves in historically relevant (for them) moments (Sahlins 1999). In sum, he treats culture as the product of people's responses to circumstances and specific history. In Sahlins's article "Two or Three Things I Know about Culture" (1999), he shields culture against abrasive treatment and total dismissal. He sees cultures coming together in ritual systems and in cosmological orders that are reproduced, elaborated, and changed by people as they actively engage with historical realities.

I am troubled by the need to recount men's stories structurally, since doing so would reduce their talk of culture to mere utility. Everyday friction that I experienced during fieldwork and that created contradictions and variations would be neglected. But Sahlins's notion that people not only share, but also are committed to, a culture helps resolve these dilemmas (1999, 410). The individual stories in this book cannot be understood unless a foundation of language concerning basic cultural categories invites us to understand practices as both stability and change.

PATRIARCHS IN THE KITCHEN

Since the 1970s, and in particular following Cynthia Nelson's (1974) article, which challenges the stereotyped images of patriarchal rule, the theme of patriarchy as integral to Islam has been replaced gradually by one that treats men and women as agents who negotiate their own survival—mostly women, in part by "bargaining with patriarchy" (Kandiyoti 1996). In the 1980s, a burst of work on women appeared; these pieces aimed at moving beyond simply debunking stereotypes to constructing theory (L. Abu-Lughod 1989). Another trend has looked at male and female roles in gender relations concurrently, particularly within the family.

Suad Joseph (1993) discusses ways in which patriarchy operates through domination by men, but also through deeply enmeshed, loving commitments between patriarchs and their female and junior kin members. According to Joseph, socialization within Arab families places a premium on connectivity, the intensive bonding of individuals through commitment and responsibility.

Recent anthropological research into the lives of men and masculinities in Egypt has significantly changed our understanding of male aspirations and practices in the family sphere. Given anthropology's past interests in the character and cycle of Egyptian lineage, the study of men seems a natural way into the ethnography of capitalism and the shape of globalization in Egyptian families. Global forces such as urbanization, migration, financial crises, political upheavals, and expanded educational and employment opportunities, as well as old and new media and information technology, all challenge and expand the boundaries of what it means to be a family man and the relationships between children and fathers.

The study of gender in relation to men, and particularly to the construction of masculinity, has created new ethnographies that include men's roles in systems of hierarchy and domination, whether in communities of study, in a national context, or in one of global conflict and inequality. The literature has moved away from a focus on women toward the study of gender relationships, including the construction of gender identity and notions of masculinity and femininity. Hence, analyzing men's and women's life strategies requires researchers to pay increased attention to ambiguity. Such an approach appeared in gender studies when biographical data on family life diverted attention from social agency and instead foregrounded agent-centered accounts that show how the family is at once modern and authentic. This scholarship allows us to grapple with individual life strategies without ironing out their inconsistencies.

In anthropology, one approach to women in the Middle East demonstrates that the social constituency of gender is fluctuating. It is concerned with bringing forth "real" individuals with particular, complex, and contradicting histories. In this type of ethnography, the style of writing expresses the dynamism, variation, and uniqueness of women's experiences. Significantly, contemporary scholarship on gender issues is founded on taking women's stories seriously. Stories are based on individual perceptions of facts; they provide knowledge of women's lives and of the gendered experiences of economic, social, and political processes. Although people's lives are lived simultaneously, stories or narratives convey patterns of experiences that show variation, contradiction, and complexity.

The gender project in the Middle East is dedicated to observing, recording, and figuring out everyday happenings. In the quest for authenticity, and to contest existing stereotypical accounts of women in the region, it is crucial to include native stories or statements, including the marginal voices of women. The pathbreaking gender research of several scholars illustrates that narratives are valuable conveyers of informa-

tion about the wealth of women's lives. Their studies make
the dynamism between creativity and agency accessible. The
complexity that surrounds these stories demonstrates that
among Middle Eastern women there are no uncomplicated
lives.

Contemporary gender research promotes the sense of live-
liness and contradiction found in everyday life as they address women's agency and self-reflection. Its reflexive writing
style includes symbolic expression and an analysis of nego-
tiated identities. Moreover, perhaps more frequently than in
other localities in the gender project, these discussions are
framed around the theory of patriarchy. The assumption is
that Islam undergirds the emphasis on patriarchy in Middle Eastern gender studies, functioning as a patriarchal orga-
nizing factor for control of the social order and, therefore, of
men's and women's social maps.

Patriarchy is undoubtedly the foundation of every part of
Arab society, and the role of women in the region is often defined within the context of patriarchal rules. In this book,
patriarchy is treated simply as the idea of the ideal Arab family—with a responsible adult male head. Patriarchy is considered a mere ideal because, as Kandiyoti (1996) argues in her
work on the role of patriarchy in Muslim society, its benefit
is unattainable for poorer women in the Middle East.

Recently there has been more emphasis on gender rather
than on family. Still, as Nicholas Hopkins (2003) reminds us,
the Arab family is a recurrent and dynamic topic. Its image
is all-embracing: a sheltered foundation within which men,
women, and children live and share whatever life brings
along. In effect, anthropologists of Egypt have always had to
cope with an indeterminate and multifaceted understanding
of the family, but the disquiet has increased greatly in recent
years as scholars have become dissatisfied with the traditional uses of the family in, for example, cultural and political studies. Traditionally, the family was seen as a highly
patterned and consistent set of representations constituted of
perceptions handed down through generations of Egyptians.

In addition, the anthropological critique took exception to the broad acceptance that the concept of consistency had gained in the public sphere, where all kinds of behaviors were seen as expressions of familial dependability. The family was proclaimed to be an essential factor for understanding Egyptian men and women's behavior and forms of interaction. This view had obvious problems when family was seen as something that people have en bloc. In scholars' attempt to add nuance to this approach, they deconstructed the concept of family, by using an idiom of power that addressed the nature of human interaction and explored the extent and kinds of family connections and practices under various social and economic conditions (L. Abu-Lughod 2013).

Scholars have posed new questions about what it means for families to go through change, especially financially induced change. They have probed deeper into temporalities in order to study change more closely and also to investigate sites where traditions were reproduced. For example, Suad Altorki provided a general historicized approach to the Egyptian household in her ethnographic analysis of middle-class family life as presented in the *Cairo Trilogy*, by Naguib Mahfouz, which shows political and economic circumstances shifting the patriarchal character of the family but still recalls specific patriarchal structures (Altorki 1999).

Recent ethnographies have provided theoretical insights into the interface between family, masculinity, patriarchy, and culture, along with new methodological orientations for understanding masculinity in its wide-ranging familial manifestations (Inhorn 2012; Ghannam 2013). In many ways, recent ethnographies on men are a reminder of Joseph's earlier work on "connectivity," in which she opened up the field by depicting the family as a collection of lives "lived together." Indeed she exposed the anthropology of family to assumptions of agency that also account for men's sensitivities and active pursuit of making a family.

With the exception of Joseph's work on connectivity and Inhorn's on conjugal love, family bonds, and care, affective

practices are almost forgotten features of Middle East studies. The depressive approach to family life in the region is
perhaps unsurprising, given the conflicts and spaces of exclu-
sion for men and women. At issue here is an intellectual un-
easiness about how to develop critical thinking about nurturing men—Muslim Arab men.

Contemporary anthropology literature concerning masculinity and the Middle East touches on men's vulnerabilities,
dependencies, and inner conflicts (see, for example, Ghannam 2002, 2013; Hafez 2012; Inhorn 2004, 2012). Farha Ghannam looked at how men participate in authentication or actively define masculinity in public and private life. She also
investigated how men discursively establish authority over
both themselves and assumptions of masculinities, which
are connected to "good grooming, nice manners, fashion-
able clothes, skill in navigating the city, assertiveness and
courage, the ability to provide for one's family, and knowledge about when to use violence to defend self, family, and
relatives" (Ghannam 2013, 24). Ghannam foregrounds biological and cultural constructions of men and the importance
of denaturalizing gendered ideologies when studying masculinities. In synthesizing existing debates on masculinity
and social constructions of men's body, Ghannam asks us
to reconsider how men, and not only women, in the Middle
East are embodied. The men in Ghannam's anthropology are
emotional, body aware, vulnerable, worried, and assertive.
For Ghannam, the most pressing problem remains not the
recognition that men collectively still have overwhelmingly
greater access to authority but, rather, men's continuing
need to be recognized as having greater authority—by both
women and men. Men's hopes, sorrows, humor, and relationships with their mothers, male relatives, neighbors, friends,
and society are vividly recounted through detailed life histories collected from families in al-Zawiya al-Hamra.

When analyzed as a social and political dimension of
men's lives, masculinity conceptualizes male identity as
variable and contested rather than as fixed and monolithic. A

subset of literature on this topic is particularly relevant here; it disputes the view that men enjoy timeless status as patriarchs or as "Arab Muslim men." Close attention to the negotiations that take place between men and women and to local lives and agency offers new paradigms for conceptualizing social change.

Anthropological and ethnographic aspects that turn up during fieldwork—such as food—offer edifying ways of questioning the complexity and contingency of masculinity. This book considers historical specificities in connection with the interplay of masculinities: in narratives of political and social change, in patterns of generational and family transformations, in labor relations, and in class structures. Historical transformation and change open up new possibilities for men and women to emerge as near reconstructions of the past or in absolutely new ways. In either case, masculinity is not entirely defined by history, a singular identity, or specific conditions.

This book is premised on masculinity's plurality, as a component of identity that does not develop according to restrictive rules but rather follows the logic of men's, and women's, everyday lives and experiences. Put crudely, men are complex selves bearing the imprint of a multitude of experiences that form their capacity to practice, to know, and to be men. By learning about their notions of what makes a man a man, we see how they interact with their families and the world to provide food and foster an ethos-informed sociability that shapes their lives.

WIT AND APPETITE

The progression of *Nurturing Masculinities* mirrors my movements in the streets, alleys, and markets of Cairo, as well as my decades of talking, cooking, and eating with my interlocutors in Egypt. Food in this book is about daily life, identity, memory, senses, aesthetics, and humor. The chapters aim to show how food, its preparation, and its consumption connect men—from different neighborhoods, age groups, classes, and educational backgrounds—to their families, their communities, and the nation at large. Chapter 1 bypasses the Arab masculinity slot and instead develops "nurturing masculinities" as a key conceptual trope for this ethnography of men and food. An anthropology attentive to food's capacity to forge ties and fulfillment has much to tell us about how men's potency is, to a great extent, also the potency of knowing, providing, and handling food. At the same time, the chapter challenges the generally strict reliance in Middle East studies on reserving the sphere of nurturance to female domesticity.

Besides being a lens for thinking about what it means to be a man and how men enact masculinity in Egypt, food can help us understand undercurrents of the 2011 revolution and the appeal and work of the Muslim Brotherhood. Chapter 2, which focuses on young members of the group, analyzes the connection between faith and pragmatism, inner conviction and conscious marketing ploy, and men's generational struggles and power shifts. In looking at the contemporary revolution, the chapter explores male outreach, the plight of stressed and hungry Egyptians, and the kind of ethical dilemmas the anthropologist faces when thinking about how to portray poverty and disillusionment.

Chapter 3 examines the long histories behind recent events, and the relation between current political change and enduring cultural practices. I revisit Mary Douglas's (1974) now-classic anthropological formulation of "deciphering a meal" in order to expand on the idea of meal recollections. Specific ingredients and dishes can reconstruct notions of manliness and thereby become memorable as sensory, as well as social, experiences. As David Sutton (2001) shows, food binds time; I draw on his work to analyze how an ingredient like samna baladi or a site like a bakery can serve as a poignant memory- and identity-making stimulant.

Phenomenological perspectives on eating, smelling, memory, sentiment, care, and nurturance provide the substance of chapter 4. It discusses gendered social roles and shows how men's manliness is inherent in being *ibn al-balad*. A discussion of conviviality and congeniality, and their aesthetic yet random association with eating and sharing food, leads to theoretical questions about men's sense of being content. For example, the men in this chapter want their children to know the ways of eating, such as tearing a small piece of bread and folding it into a cat's ear before scooping from a common dish.

The concluding chapter raises major issues one last time. As I wrote during the white nights of summer in Oslo in 2014, the Muslim Brotherhood government was ousted by what the media calls the largest street protest in history. A new military government was sworn in, and one of my main interlocutors, an officer, called to ask when I was coming back to Cairo to celebrate and eat.

CHAPTER I

NURTURING MASCULINITIES

Everyone who has been in love or built a family knows that there are things, essential things, that money can't buy.

ARTHUR KLEINMAN, "THE ART OF MEDICINE" (2012)

IN 2011, AS I READ THROUGH field notes from decades of research in the Middle East and write this account, food prices are rising around the world and angry populations are gathering in squares, streets, and gardens. They are using the vocabulary of democracy in their demands for justice and dignity. They are creating new spaces where new orders can be imagined. A striking feature connecting these spontaneous movements is that people bring along food and water to share with others.

In Cairo and close to the barricades in Tahrir Square, I witnessed extraordinary weeks of human drama played out in public spaces, where notions of the gifts being circulated gave me renewed insight into relationships in the Middle East. Of course, these events were fragmentary and evanescent, but this ethnographic moment inspired me to look and think again about forms of sociability and the complexities of living in Egypt. Surely, many of us who work in the Middle East know that daily outreach is an old story in the region.

THE STUFF OF LIFE

Some of the most unassuming yet compelling aspects of the social fabric are found in what is here called the "stuff of life." These are the small occurrences and gestures that make up Egyptian society. The stuff of life is found in the gestures, words, things, events, surroundings, and passing moods and atmospheres that provide people with a sense of satisfaction and pleasure in their everyday lives. This chapter shows how the stuff of life is brought into sharper relief when juxtaposed with masculinities and food. I bring together inputs that are organized around aspects of the stuff of life, a structure that is intended to define, develop, and contribute to a broader understanding of men's food worlds.

This chapter develops a specific view of the stuff of life among Egyptian men, based on a perspective drawn from field notes and interviews. Along with exploring the stuff of life, I review my decades of fieldwork in the Middle East, which challenges the distorted image of Middle Eastern men as sullen, affectionless, and sunk in relational poverty. I explore Egyptian men's daily food experiences in order to go from previous ideas of what manhood is or what it feels like to an interpretation of what it does. Nurturing masculinities are revealed in men's notions of manliness, particularly those concerning the provisioning, sharing, and articulation of food. Indeed, as one man told me, "The deal is the food." A representative sample of observations and quotations from my Cairo field notes, collected over a span of more than thirty years, gives a sense of these attitudes:

Spent the day in Bulaq with Farouk, his mother, and friends. They told me that it's all about satisfying food, togetherness, and a quick wit. NOVEMBER 15, 1980

Food in Egypt has to [be] satisfying, filling and shared in agreeable company. It's time for anthropology to pay closer attention to stuff that gives our interviewees a sense of pleasure. JANUARY 10, 1998

FIGURE 5. Nurturing masculinity, 2012.

> Tahrir Square today. Everyone brought food to share. What a party this has become: I [am] sitting here on the pavement sharing recipes with a family from Sayyida Zeinab. There was a lot of talk about filling, satisfying, and celebratory dishes. FEBRUARY 9, 2011

> If I think of general ideas about men and food, one idea in particular stands out. Egyptian men feel that food has to be satisfying and the company has to be warm and enjoyable. Economy is in very deep crisis, still I keep hearing my interlocutors say, "Egypt is the blessed country, things will go well." MARCH 4, 2013

One of anthropology's most significant aspects lies in how it addresses underlying values in people's relationships to one another and to their surroundings. This point supports the idea of culture as practice, which I draw on throughout this book, because particular values have critical consequences at moments of crisis, like the current political and economic uncertainty in Egypt.

THE MASCULINE SLOT

All things that a man owns hold him far more than he holds them. SIGRID UNDSET, *KRISTEN LAVRANSDATTER*

Men are often forgotten in my own and other scholars' writings about compassion and caregiving in the Middle East. We know about the long-term daily charitable giving, rescue, protection, shelter, and ordinary gestures of kindness essential to the daily scheme of interaction in the Middle East. Yet men's feelings of compassion and practices of care remain insufficiently addressed. A close scrutiny of men's foodways raises interesting questions about fluid associations between codified masculinity and masculine practices. Such an examination reveals something about men's capacity to construct connections with others, and the life course of concern that uncertainties produce.

Marcia Inhorn (2012) correlates Middle Eastern forms of patriarchy with kinship practices and Islam (the family patriarch) on the one hand, and with in vitro fertilization centers and patriarchal connectivities (male commitment) on the other. Identified as "emergent," this understanding of masculinities reveals not just the patriarchal dimensions of a mode of social life but also the local and emotional world it underpins. Inhorn makes the case for emphasizing particularity over typology: "It is crucial to develop new theoretical approaches that, when applied to ethnographic cases of real men's lives, do not reify them into particular 'types' of men but instead account for their nuanced and constantly evolving responses to their changing social worlds" (62).

In *The New Arab Man: Emergent Masculinities, Technologies, and Islam in the Middle East*, Inhorn takes up Raewyn W. Connell's (1995) "dynamics of masculinities" and expands on Connell's four masculine varieties—hegemonic, complicitous, marginalized, and subordinate—in her analysis of the Arab patriarch (2012, 41–62).[1] I follow Inhorn's ar-

1. Raewyn W. Connell was formerly Robert W. Connell.

gument that men must be studied as "lived masculinities on the local level" (62). My male interlocutors demonstrated on-the-ground masculine practices and concerns. Food activities carried out by men form a fundamental component of the ideology of gender and social life in contemporary Egypt—gendered space, gendered work, and gendered relationships tied to everyday food concerns. While the importance of power and the hierarchal aspects of food and gender need to be recognized, here I am most interested in the masculine modalities that food generates in men's lives.

In making her argument about masculine distinctions, Susie Kilshaw (2009, 189) uses Michael Kimmel to define masculinity "more by what one is not, than who one is." But my interlocutors speak about who they are; they cite virtues such as gallantry, clearness, conservatism, joviality, and manliness. An *ibn al-balad* is a man who is committed to preserving Egyptian values, but he is also flexible and adaptable. He loves a good joke; more importantly, he knows how to laugh at himself. He is aware of his strength and manliness. He is the man of the house, with complete authority over, and an expectation of obedience from, his wife and family, and he has total responsibility for his family's well-being. For an *ibn al-balad*, food symbolizes his ability to fulfill his obligation to pamper his family. Hence, the masculinity described in this book is one in which identities are bound up with distinct food values and patterns of behavior.

This study of masculinity looks at the ability of anthropology to investigate masculinity and food in order to contextualize what else is happening in the lives of men doing what men do. What I call nurturing masculinities, namely, men's food talk and their efforts to care for loved ones, problematizes the hitherto exclusive link between femininity and food in Egypt. Indeed, it displays food talk and practices as "lived masculinities" (Inhorn 2012). Food, like religion and politics, involves morality, tasks, controversy, and convention—notions of human involvement that cannot always be classified as gender based.

In keeping with Inhorn's new picture of the Arab man and

emerging masculinities in a rapidly changing Middle East, this book puts forward the notion of masculine action as a way of nurturing and as a form of caregiving. Caregiving is embedded in practices, discourses, controversies, and principles that are not always easily categorized. By drawing attention to some of the less obvious ways in which care is practiced, expressed, acquired, and experienced, I attempt to contribute to a nuanced interpretation and examination of men's domestic sentiments.

Arthur Kleinman (2009, 3) calls caregiving "a defining moral practice." Hence, in employing caregiving to make an argument about nurturing masculinity, I use Kleinman's process of practice that creates caregivers: "It is a moral practice that makes caregivers, and at times even the care-receivers, more present and thereby fully human" (293). This process is significant when concerned with the caregiving implications that food reproduces in men's practice. Thus, food can communicate and assemble two elements: caregiving and masculinity. The argument of the book is essentially about a dynamic social process of how men respond to what happens in the life of the household.

Food provisioning, one of the ways that food contributes to caregiving as a way for men to be men, is not only a necessity, but is also linked with an overall sense of masculinity and men's relationships. Consequently, the associations between food and masculinity are complicated. Important dynamics reveal food's ethnographically particular masculinity-constructing aspects, which can serve as salient illustrations of gender issues in the scholarship of social activism. Gender research on the relationship between women as agents of social activism investigates women's activities during global and national crises, providing insights into how women "pick up the pieces" and turning up the volume on their voices, knowledge, and responses to political upheaval, social unrest, and economic uncertainty (see, for example, Baron 2005; Naguib 2010; E. Thompson 2000). These studies have revealed women's remarkable resilience during crises.

Studies of crisis in the Middle East are mostly accounts of political, economic, and military events. Less familiar are the stories of how men strive to protect the material shell of family life. Although Egyptian men do not nurture home life in the sense of providing daily child care, cooking, or cleaning, they play an active role in the production of domestic space and relationships, which my interlocutors experienced differently from women. In concentrating on food concerns and practices that directly affect men and women's lives and identities, this book explores what may be inferred about men's ideas about women and femininity, about constructions of masculinity and difference, and therefore about some past and contemporary societal changes in Egyptian society.

Men's foodways and their daily lives may be understood in the context of a wider ideology of obligation that contrasts with one that defines male, as well as female, ideals and expressed differences in society. Indeed, there are divergences between generations, classes, ideals of masculinity, and forms of patriarchy, but it is possible to bring together, through food, some of the spaces in which Egyptian men of different classes and ages move, and some of the ways in which they aim to fulfill roles as providers of food for their families. Ethnographies of food features in men's daily chores help clarify contemporary redefinitions of masculinity, domesticity, and gender roles, as well as the meaning of statements such as "A man has his integrity," "One has to be a man (ragel)," and "The life of men is complicated." There are two reasons, then, that I have attempted to recover the masculine in everyday life. First, Middle Eastern gender studies has mostly treated masculinity in its patriarchal and militarized forms. (For exceptions, see Joseph 1999, Inhorn 2012, and Ghannam 2013.) Second, Arab Muslim men are invisible in most histories and ethnographies of daily chores. Men's roles as agents of domesticity and the ways in which they value ordinary, everyday practices, whether regarding food or caring for the young, have been marginalized and neglected.

How can we talk about food activities and masculinity?

How do men see the world of food and its place in their daily routine? What are their needs and desires regarding food? What role does food play in maintaining and shaping their notions of masculinity? These are the kinds of questions to ask when trying to understand the social worlds that food builds for men. By paying close attention to the language of food that men use when they talk about life, perhaps we can dispel the illusion that Arab men are adequately explained by reference to patriarchy.

In this attempt to offer insight into enactments of masculinities, food's materiality and social context impart meaning to the stuff and practice, and also to the ways in which men live their manliness beyond the masculine slot. My arguments about masculinity and food in Egypt depend on translations between notions of the nature of manliness and ordinary practices.

OF MANHOOD AND FOOD

Thomas Hobbes ([1651] 1958) writes in *Leviathan* that the natural state of humankind is that of war and strife. Humanity, Hobbes argues, is inherently drawn to aggression and the subjugation of others. Michael Herzfeld's (1985) portrayal of Greek men in a mountain village seems to relate to Hobbes's "natural state." In his now-classic book *The Poetics of Manhood*, Herzfeld emphasizes a type of performativity that links masculinity with the state of being a man. His interlocutors were men who were "good at" being men when they stole and then boasted about it. They stole because they were hungry and because they were being "eaten" by others. Michael Gilsenan's (1996) interlocutors in *Lords of the Lebanese Marches* were men who were men when they skillfully recounted past "dirty deeds." Their accounts were meant to illustrate how men in a Lebanese province tried to make sense of their lives and senses of identity, and how they claimed their manhood as control shifted and statuses were challenged. Male behavior emerged from verbal jousting and violent acts.

Since the work of Herzfeld and Gilsenan, the anthropological study of male behavior, physical and verbal, has redefined what its facts are, what it does, and to what it is comparable. As accounts of masculinity have expanded into different areas, the field has shifted its emphasis to expressive and performative culture. The shift has been particularly fruitful in studies of cultures characterized by a good deal of display and talk. Mathew Gutmann (1997, 396) identifies broad definitions of masculinity within anthropology— "anything that men think and do," "anything men think and do to be men," and "anything that women are not"—and he notes that "some men are . . . 'more manly' than other men." Indeed, my interlocutors have said all the above.

Men, like women, are positioned in a complex system of power relationships. Some men struggle to maintain or improve their positions with regard to others. To be or not to be a man is then less a question of cultural concepts than of particular ways of interaction and being in the world. Consequently, attention to individual men is required.

If ethnographers used all varieties of reflexivity in practice, they might be able to let go a little of what Donna Haraway (1988) calls the "God-trick" of science. We must listen and find a place for individuals and their actions; this is when narratives are essential. Inhorn's work on emerging masculinities is so appealing because it illuminates the importance of men's most intimate worlds and of the fine details of their meanings.

After dislocating masculinity from patriarchy, scholars have been struck by the extent to which masculinities emerge in unexpected settings and under surprising circumstances. Sherine Hafez (2012) traces Deniz Kandiyoti's "patriarchal bargain" to argue that men, too, bargain for their choices. Hafez rethinks authoritarian expressions of masculinity and decides that changing power positions between males are more critical in masculinity constructions than she had previously argued.

Samer Shehata's *Shop Floor Culture and Politics in Egypt* (2012), which concerns a group of male factory workers, notes how the production of things is a production of identity and social relations. While neither masculinity nor gender is the subject of interest, the author shows how ordinary workers— "unremarkable in many respects"—conceive of and practice their relationships (2). Shehata explains that he wanted to understand "what they know and how they live" (2). Everyday commensality over vegetables, fava beans, falafel, bread, and glasses of tea with sugar are just some of the ways shop floor workers regulate their time and construct their identities and their relationships to one another: "Tea not only provides workers with a momentary break, a short escape from boredom of work, allowing them to temporarily leave the side of their machines, it also provides a chance to socialize with mates, gossip, talk, and even clown around" (26–27).

Shehata's ethnography is useful for this discussion, since his analysis of eating and drinking patterns among men suggests some abstract social rules for understanding male spaces and social practices. *Shop Floor Culture* gives a clear sense of how food provides a powerful channel of human exchange that expresses and distinguishes among kin, friend, rival, power, and powerlessness. This same sense of food held sway in the everyday worlds of my interlocutors.

Individual relationships and broad patterns of societal relationships are displayed in different ways through food provisioning and consumption. Food is a substance of care as much as an agent of control, as Carole Counihan (1988) argues in her discussions on the power and influence acquired by Florentine women through their productive and nurturing food activities. Counihan stresses the important constituting force that food has in women's lives; women are empowered through their "feeding" activities (54), which provide food-centered ethnographies that "give voice" (1) to women.

But as a field, food studies suffers from a prestige problem.

As Jon Holtzman (2009, 53) notes, "Though well-established anthropological subjects, such as kinship, sexuality, and religion, have the advantage of decades of scholarship concerned with overcoming our cultural constructions . . . the anthropology of food has not always moved convincingly beyond Western constructions of food." Holtzman argues for an anthropology that can show how the ethnography of food produces meaningful social analysis. He extends Sutton's (2001, 3) discussions of how food studies, in general, is perceived as "scholarshiplite."

In his book *Remembrance of Repasts: An Anthropology of Food and Memory* (2001), Sutton tells the story of an Oxford don's response to Sutton's planned study: "Food and memory? Why would anyone want to remember anything they have eaten?" (1). At first Sutton was upset by the humiliating snap, but after experiencing a dinner at Oxford High Table, "where a profusion of potatoes and overboiled vegetables was presented and just as quickly whisked away" (1), he understood the don's reaction. Sutton was astonished by the "stillness" that met his search through the anthropological literature on memory for any treatment of food, and I continue to find stillness in searching for the treatment of food and men—and indeed, also of women and food—in ethnographies of Middle Eastern lifeworlds.

My approach is to turn up the volume on men's voices in order to hear how they define their manliness, and many other things, according to responsibilities near the kitchen. To paraphrase one man: "It is shameful for a man not to give his wife enough money for the food, and not to come home at least once a week with seasonal fruits for the children. You know, I turn the key to my home and I hear my daughter ask, 'What did you get me today, *ya baba?*'" Concern about bringing home a food favorite for the children is a major theme among my interlocutors. This concern dovetails with men's aspirations to maintain a traditional Egyptian family with moral values.

Why and what can food tell us about being a man in contemporary Egypt? The stories my interlocutors told about themselves through food reflect notions of the self, personal goals, and understandings of close and societal obligations and relationships.

The question of how masculinity is lived requires an ethnographic answer, one using the particularities of men—as sons, brothers, husbands, and fathers—and their lives to understand how they negotiate their identities against the backdrop of tales about food. The stories included here focus on the narrative creation of the self through the vehicle of food. Men are shown inside the company of their immediate families, inside their parental love, and inside their intimacy, which frequently leads to self-reflection. There are no constructions of masculinity, or at least not the whole edifice.

Toward the end of my fieldwork in Cairo in the winter of 2013, I interviewed Fahmi Hassan, a forty-year-old farmer who turned to gardening and eventually opened his own flower shop in a relatively upscale neighborhood of Cairo. He complained about how food expenses were destroying "the spirit" of the traditional Egyptian family. During the conversation, the subject of "the role of men" came up. I asked him about the causes of broken families, and he listed several items, including "a spiritually broken and confused role for men." The man is the primary caretaker and socializer of the family: "He provides the means for his wife to be able to nourish his family." True, he continued, a young man today will look for a wife who has a career. His oldest daughter has an education and a steady career: "Without two salaries, you just cannot make a home." Nonetheless, some conventions had to be observed: "One must be a man, and a family man has proper values and behavior. There are expectations from family and society, and a man must honor his obligations."

Fahmi got his inspiration from the gardens he tended, "nearly like my children," and from the flowers in his shop: "There is a cycle in life, and each man is given a portion. Not more, but also not less." A man, he explained, wants his family to bud full of life. When a man cannot meet his ob-

FIGURE 6. Fahmi and Nabawi Hassan with their youngest daughter, Heba, 2103.

ligations to nourish his family, "like the flowers they will wither." He considered ongoing changes in how Egyptians eat, linking the transformations to what he called a "deterioration in society's respect for the nourishment that God provides."

He continued: "I thank God every day that I can feed my family. When the madam cooks everyday nourishing food for the children, it brings everyone together. We all eat from the same pot." He looked down on his callused hands and added, "I try to do two things: follow God's wishes and feed my family." Slowly he lifted his head, grinned, and said, "Don't look so sad, *ya doctora*. I also try to watch as much football as I can." As Fahmi explained, a man's ability to provide for his family involves more than simple consumption; rather, it fundamentally symbolizes and structures the man's identity, his aspirations, and his relationship to his family. For Fahmi, feeding his family was about more than merely eating; at many levels, food created proper behavior that shaped his role as a family man.

My interviewees' perceptions were formed by the times in which they lived. Perceptions of time and transformation were connected with the men as subjects and agents of history—how they think, feel, and react to their world. Like the ritual symbols described by Victor Turner (1969), food activities, symbolizing the value of being a caretaker, have both an emotional and an instrumental position in my interlocutors' ranges of meaning. The emotional position connects their sense of being a man with an intangible collective entity. The instrumental position concerns religion and social work, particularly mobilization for food justice.

My encounters and conversations exposed a spectrum of piety and ideas about men doing what men do as men. Their accounts and activities demonstrated how "emergent masculinities" (Inhorn 2012) are processual and impinge on everyday life in meaningful ways. Food talk and practices appear to be driven by obligation and traditional sensibility, but also by personal choice and outward expressions of gender and generational roles, relations, and transformations.

Food should be seen as having radical potential for creating different gender representations, concerns, and values, as well as a way to explore forms of masculine representation in the Middle East. The key analytical question for the anthropology of food and gender might be, how do men do what men do by creating new or different meanings for forms of practice? For anthropology, men's food practices revive questions of public and private spheres, household chores, and practice as analytical units. These questions raise further ones about the extent to which food can guide an understanding of how men think about themselves, women, community, and the world. The anthropology of food and masculinities can be enormously creative in developing new, critical ways to analyze food activities as ideology, as culture, and as potentially transformative societal and emotional possibilities for men and women.

EAT LIKE AN EGYPTIAN

The anthropology of food frequently points out the ways in which cooking and eating are central to cosmologies, worldviews, and ways of life. One interesting extension of such work is the focus on how food is gendered by its negative or positive values. Paul Stoller (1997, 86) does not write about gender, but he does ask anthropologists to reconsider their hang-ups by "dusting off" cultural life in order to clean up ethnography. But he warns that too much dusting "kicks up clouds that obscure one's vision" (87). Picking up on Stoller's dusting metaphor, I think that an appreciation of sense modalities overturns our fixed notions about Egyptian men, and Middle Eastern men in general, and makes us reconsider men's sensory worlds, which are brought about through forms of aesthetics and humor. A sense of humor and aesthetics, overlapping fields of everyday sociability, suggest alternative ways of interpreting men's food experiences.

My attention was first drawn to the topic of humor and aesthetics during a study of junior officers in the Egyptian army. Early in the 1990s, Samir Nazif did his service: "I was excited about it, but so disappointed when I joined. The army was not an army. We were a gang of young, very bored men who missed our mother's cooking and joking with our chums." Like most Egyptians, he had to choose between three years in the police or one year in the army. He was more fortunate than others:

> I was just out of medical school, so I practiced as a doctor in the army, and as you see I stayed on, which also means I get to talk to lots of men about many very different life problems and their deep anxieties about doing the right thing. I can tell you a thing or two about the Egyptian man.

He had a lot to say, and I listened politely to his stories from the barracks. Then one day he remarked that I was not taking notes or asking "difficult questions." Somewhat relieved by his observation, I said something to the effect that I could not see how listening to stories about military men or speaking to men in the service was relevant to my project on Egyptian men and food. I could not see how the ethos of militarism would make it possible for them to discuss something as ordinarily civilian as food. Outraged, Samir responded, "Military men are very anxious about food and water. First because we are posted in forsaken places. Then there is the issue of our family back home and if they have enough food on the table." My feeble response regarding military men and food convinced him that I needed direction in my "men and food chase," as he called it.

Samir became an enthusiastic and key interlocutor during my fieldwork. He talked about how men demand forms of care, security, and rights that make it possible for them to be men: "Egyptian society is not only tough for women, it is also hard on men." A man had to assert responsibility and sacrifice or be "subjected to society and his family, like women are." As a doctor, Samir examined not only hurting bodies but also "very wounded souls." He was especially concerned about young married officers stationed far from home, who complain about the strain of not being with their families. The problem was less about missing their families, which they did, than about being away from obligations: "They complain about the obligations. But when they don't have them they worry. Catch-22 [he said in English]." This puzzled me. He continued:

> As a military man, I am like any other *ibn balad*. A man is a man when he can feed his family. The family order is as important as it is necessary for him to be the man of the family. A man thinks that the home is disquieted by his absence. He feels order and responsibility when he is there to see that food is on the table. A home for me is the place where I like the food and the people.

Smiling shyly, he added, "And . . . my wife likes the way I like her food."

I wanted to know whether he chose the daily menu, whether his wife did the shopping, and who did the cooking. He admitted to being "particular" about his food, and his wife infantilized his tastes by teasing him: "She tells me that I am only happy with my mama's cooking." Was that true? After a long pause, he nodded. But he was quick to add:

> I am *ibn al-balad*, but I am not *si-Sayyid*. That time is over.
> My wife has a job. She might also be tired when she comes
> home. It is not like before. I cannot expect to come home
> and find her waiting like in the old movies. Anyway, with all
> the traffic we usually don't eat at the same time. It's not like
> when I was a boy and we all had our meal together, cooked
> by my mother's beautiful hands.

Si-Sayyid, "master," is the short name of the family patriarch, Al-Sayyid Ahmad Abd al-Jawad, in Naguib Mahfouz's *Cairo Trilogy*. Called *si-Sayyid* by his wife and neighbors, he represents the authoritarian Egyptian man who rules his household with harsh discipline. In *si-Sayyid*'s house, the wife, maid, and daughters prepare the food. *Si-Sayyid* sits at the table alone and starts eating; he then invites his sons. Behind them, his wife and daughters watch and serve them until they finish their meal. Only then can the women taste the food they have prepared, as they finish what the men have left over. The point Samir made is that although he admits to being difficult about his food, he is not a dominating man. While he does not take a primary role in food preparation, he takes considerable interest in his wife's efforts.

Samir describes himself as "*ibn balad* [in] following the ways of taking care of my family." I first met him in the 1990s, while he was a student and I was carrying out fieldwork in a couple of popular historic quarters in Cairo. Over the years, he has talked to me about how his neighborhood roots urge him as "a genuine *ibn balad*": chivalrous, generous, smart, and "light-blooded" (quick witted).

Consequently, regardless of Samir's experiences as a man, he models himself on the multiple nature of his and his significant others' experiences of themselves, both in concrete material ways and in more gender-based, affective ways that may arise from contexts having little to do with manliness and more to do with food. To be chivalrous, generous, and clever takes the gender divide for granted. Demonstrations of manhood are thus lived out in a material and public world. In *Still Life: Hopes, Desires, and Satisfactions* (2011), Henrietta Moore rethinks human potentialities and people's ways of "retain[ing] a regard for what is distinctively human about being and doing the world" (24). In this chapter, the idea of a man being a man relates to the potential changes that food practices might bring and the possibilities for new ways of regarding men's control while "being and doing the world."

The "modern" family structure that Samir spoke about reflects an expansive use of the sharing of food and sentimental ties with his wife. Food was both a visceral and emblematic sign of him as a modern Egyptian man. It was a medium he uses to explain his relationship. Both Samir and his wife nurture a culinary repertoire of typical dishes that include his (and her) childhood favorites.

Food also connects husband and wife. In somewhat puzzling ways, Samir redeemed the same "old days" that he had referred to as being "like the old movies." However peculiar this contrast, it was typical of many of my interlocutors. Samir's account highlights not only his male sense of a breadwinner's obligations but also its affective aspects, which are often linked with and modeled after recollections from past experiences. For alongside his wish to feed his family well and often, he discussed effects that were profoundly emotional.

Anthropologists are redrawing masculinity in important ways. Rather than being seen as a function of dominance, virility, or vulnerability, masculinity is viewed through connections, fluidity, and transformation. Although we should avoid a culturalistic approach, which, as Annika Rabo (2006, 48) explains, "obscures more than it illuminates," the essence of the stories we collect requires insight into social and linguistic environments. The crucial question is, how can we, as interpreters of other lives, learn to ask questions that interest our interviewees, rather than relying on neat, convenient labels of culture? Feminist and gender studies of women in the Middle East have succeeded in bringing forward a sensitivity to "other" women's lives, which are far richer and more complex than earlier narratives about the region suggested. The question is whether writing women's ethnographies in a voice other than that of the interlocutors constructs or invents otherness and difference in Middle Eastern men.

This genealogy of concepts of food provisioning, in Foucauldian terms, links the giving of nourishment and the practices of everyday life with great sentiment. The everyday social world of meals is an enactment of men's identities and relations, especially when meals are taken with the women and children for whom they care. Janet Carsten (1995, 234) writes about kinship in a Malay fishing community from the perspective of the kitchen hearth. She gives the hearth a "female structure" that reproduces kinship, since kin are those who gather to eat food cooked in the same household. Carsten's compelling ethnography addresses the anthropology of the relationship between hearth and nurture. She shows how feeding is a means of incorporation, of making similar those who are different or not related by blood. Women accomplish this task. In Carsten's book based on her research, *The Heat of the Hearth: The Process of Kinship in a Malay Fishing Community* (1997), she looks closely at "feeding, hospitality, exchanges, marriage, children, fostering, and grand-parenthood—all the ways in ways in which Malay people on the island of Langkawi become kin." As the subtitle of her book suggests, "Kinship and personhood in Langkawi have to be understood in processual terms"; specifically, "identity . . . is both given at birth through ties of procreation, but perhaps more importantly, it is also acquired throughout life by living together in one house and sharing food" (4).

I suggest that ties of procreation are an avenue for rethinking the female-male nurturing divide in the Middle East. The concept of procreation brings men to the hearth. It tells us something else about how men see themselves as nurturers. Thinking more deeply about men's "ties of procreation" through food opens up our discussion of masculinity in interesting ways.

DO LIKE A MAN

Human struggles over, and connections between, providing food and caring are established culturally as well as politically. At root is the idea that men—husbands and fathers—draw authority from their ability to control the distribution of food to their dependents. Thus, a point of contention in societies based on such authority is the failure of men to meet their obligations to their dependents. The work of scholars such as Suad Joseph (1983, 1993), Diane Singerman (1997), Farha Ghannam (2013), and Homa Hoodfar (1997) provides insights into the ways in which patriarchy operates through male domination, but also through deeply enmeshed, loving commitments between Arab patriarchs and their female and junior kin members. There is, Joseph (1983, 60–61) tells us, plenty of evidence that both women and men are active in their pursuit of shaping the family life that emerges from their quotidian engagements. Her studies point out that socialization within Arab families places a premium on connectivity, the intense bonding of individuals through love, involvement, commitment, and responsibility.

This image of bonding is in line with my argument about masculinities and nurturing. "Obligation" implies a curious human act, one that is both supplement and remainder. It can alter the kinds of relations people have with others. Anthropologists distinguish between life as lived, life as experienced, and a life as told. Somewhere here is the commonsense boundary between self and world that makes it possible to examine individual identities as "mobile sites of contradiction and disunity, a node where various discourses temporarily intersect in particular ways" (Kondo 1990, 47).

But what else is implied by self and world regarding the intersection of men and food? Men speak about a strong gender component of the cooking and serving of food. One man, who claimed to be a very good cook, said that he was the youngest of five brothers and used to shop and help his mother in the kitchen. When he got married, he said, his wife was very impressed. Indeed, Egyptian men claim that they are famous for shopping for the best meat and fruit and for never buying anything in small quantities. "The man has to come home with both arms carrying food," a café owner told me. Sutton (2001, 21) writes about similar male approaches to shopping: on the island of Kalymnos, men and women are expected to be good at bargaining, but men have their "honor" to consider, and will thus wave aside any cost concerns once they have decided on a particular food purchase.

I found similar accounts in Sutton's ethnography. In one story, a woman relays how her husband simply disregards "the additional trifle" (2001, 21). Likewise, Mustafa Hashim, a taxi driver, told me that his wife teases him, saying that the butcher is a thief who gets away with overcharging only "old-school men" like him: "*El madam* says he looks at me and cuts a larger chunk. I come home, and she looks at it, and I know what she is going to say before she even thinks it: '*Ya salam, ya Mustafa.*' I suppose you just waived the extra five kilos as if it is nothing?" What does he say then? "What can I say? She knows I have my pride. An Egyptian man is a family man. He cannot just buy a slice of meat and two green beans. Then she prepares something for the children and me." His wife, whom he, like my other interlocutors, calls "*el madam*," is a real lady of the house, *sett el beit*.

I tried to find out more: "Did you marry her because of her cooking?" Mustafa began a familiar account:

My father died when I was fourteen. I started driving his Peugeot taxi. Imagine[,] I did not have a driving license. My mother worried. But we, she and I, had four others to feed. Every time a traffic policeman stopped me to ask for the license, I told them my story. With the exception of one, they all felt sorry for me. Egyptians have compassion [*rahma*]. But there was this guy, a policeman. He made me drive his wife and children around for a whole day of shopping. Then he let me go. God forgive him. In this world, you have to take things easy and put your trust in God. You know, I am lucky because my mother prays for me.

Life at home got more and more expensive. He drove all day and night: "I will never let this car go. Without the Peugeot, I could never have sent all my sisters and brothers to university and later married them off with dignity."

When it was time for him to get married, his mother and younger sister took charge: "They are both like the midwives of the neighborhood. Nothing passes them by. They know everything about everyone." Obviously, his mother and sisters had been watching a special woman for a long time: the daughter of the shopkeeper on the corner. Mustafa laughs, "Like everything Egyptian, it became a soap opera." His mother and sister convinced him to go and talk to the woman's father. He stalled. Then, while preparing his glass of tea in the morning, his mother announced that she and the woman's father were in agreement. Curious about his reaction, I said something about arranged marriages. He replied, "This lady has a higher education. A teacher. What would she want with me? I did not finish my preparatory schooling." He described unbearable nagging by his mother and sister—"the first thing I heard in the morning and the last thing I heard before going to sleep." Finally, Mustafa agreed to go to see the father: "I told him what my mother left out. That I left school, that I drive the taxi, that I am straightforward. Then I told him before anything is decided I want to say all this to his daughter." He then met his future wife: "I said quickly hello. Then I went straight to the point."

Now I was really very curious. He continued:

To tell you the truth, I went there with my mother and sister. All the way both women are telling me what to say and what not to say. How to behave. I say yes, yes. The father opens the door. We are made very welcome. You know Egyptians. Coffee, Pepsi, tea, gateaux, this and that. I look at my future wife and say everything my mother and sister told me not to say. That I am a man who does not know how to give a woman compliments. I don't do the flirting thing. I am not going to tell her that her eyes are this or that. That I am not an educated [person] like her. My mother started to say something. But I told her to let me finish. I went on to say that I am that kind of man that does not want his wife to work outside. If she thinks she wants me, I will make sure she never lacks anything. That there will always be the best cuts of meat, freshest vegetables, fruits, and softest bread in the house.

Mustafa married Hoda four weeks after this episode: "*Tota tota*, and the story is finished." A year after this conversation, I was invited to meet his mother, Hoda, and the rest of the family. Mustafa's story continues in a later chapter.

CARING LIKE A MAN

It was after observing men like Ahmad Tawil and Hussein Maher and listening to Samir's and Mustafa's food concerns that I started to think about the themes of masculinity and care. Certain obligations associated with men are generalized by society. A man has to provide food for his family. Occasionally, he should come home with something special to eat. During religious or public holidays, he is expected to take the family to partake in the festivities. And so on. Prevalent though it is, caregiving and affective gestures are never entirely simple matters for either women or men. They involve multiple acts of affection and authority. I have come to regard men's food activities as not entirely separate from women's.

As Janice Boddy (2007, 14) writes, "Studies about women are never only about women." So it is that men's stories are never only about men. Bringing men's stories to the fore shows how stories challenge generalizations about social structure and culture, along with stereotypes about Arab Muslim men. Stories help us avoid the temptation to oppose ethnographies about women and ethnographies about men. Indeed, feminist literature by Arab and non-Arab scholars on gender roles and relationships has seen robust growth and generated interesting discussions beyond stereotypical gender relations in the region.

In many cases, feminist interpretations and accounts of masculinities are mutually reinforcing, especially in the context of domestic care, one of the key concepts with which I examine men's foodways. Masculine identities take many forms, and are articulated in numerous sites of cultural, social, emotional, religious, political, economic, and gendered expression. The important point here is that scholars too often try to contain or separate ideas about men, manliness, and masculinities from men's ordinary, daily interactions with women and children. By bringing together the spaces that Egyptian men of different classes, politics, and ages inhabit, along with their food concerns and their struggles to feed their families during both stable and tumultuous times, my discussion provides a new density and definition to the complex negotiations of gender and other social allocations that underpin social and cultural continuities. I think that men, manliness, and masculinities, taken together, help us understand how contemporary redefinitions of Egyptian domesticity, gender roles, and concepts like "husband" and "father" intersect faith, tradition, obligations, and the modern world, and how the intersection can be seen in food activities. The following chapters expose a layered view of men's caregiving through life histories that illustrate how food is an object of cultural and gendered formulations that challenge preconceived ideas about the masculine slot.

CHAPTER 2

FOOD FOR FAITH

Work without hope draws nectar in a sieve
And hope without an object cannot live.

SAMUEL TAYLOR COLERIDGE, "WORK WITHOUT HOPE"

THE SOCIETY OF THE MUSLIM BROTHERS is the oldest
and largest Islamist movement in Egypt. It was established
in 1928 by Hassan el-Banna, a primary school teacher. From
the start, el-Banna demanded from Egyptians a stronger commitment to the welfare of their community and an aware-
ness of those less fortunate than themselves (Davis and Robinson 2012; Naguib 1996). While the movement has always
had a steady flow of recruits in rural areas, it more recently
has experienced increasing involvement from young urban
and university-educated men who have deep concerns about
the arrogance and corruption of those in power (Singerman
2004). The young Brothers became particularly visible during Egypt's "Friday Day of Rage," January 28, 2011, when activists used Facebook, YouTube, and text messages to organize protests against rising food prices, police brutality, and
governmental corruption. Although not the first time Egyptians had protested these ills, the demonstrations, and the
popular rage they channeled, managed to oust President
Hosni Mubarak and his government. Tahrir Square became
the epicenter for people's demands for bread, dignity, and justice. I watched as Muslim Brotherhood youth surrounded the

FIGURE 7. Muslim Brothers distributing bread during the Egyptian revolution, Tahrir, 2011.

square, under banners with the slogan "Religion is for God; the Country is for All." They ensured that food, especially bread, as well as water and bandages, reached protesters.

This chapter looks at the youth branch of the Brotherhood and its prospects for social change through food. It inquires into the Brothers' social efforts regarding food activism and how they make their influence felt in society's fabric. I knew about the Brotherhood's social service efforts from my anthropological research on its business ethics and welfare involvements. In my first attempt to study Arab Muslim male lives and aspirations, in the 1990s, I looked at the philanthropic and economic lives of the most successful Brotherhood businessmen, calling them "men of commitment" (Naguib 1996). As commodity prices rose and food riots spread across the world in 2007 and 2008, I decided to return to Egypt to study the food protests. I wondered whether Brotherhood businessmen were involved in food welfare programs.

As with my previous research, I was fortunate to gain ethnographic access to the group's social work. I became interested in its vision and efforts for food justice when one of my previous interlocutors, a doctor and Brother whom I have known for close to fifteen years, suggested I look more closely at the group's food activities. He acknowledged that he had never really thought about the "food question" until he worked in a clinic where many of his patients suffered from nutritional deficiencies and could afford only "to fill up their calories with bad-quality, subsidized bread."

PARADIGMS OF FAITH AND FOOD

I had no idea how to go about researching the Brotherhood's food projects except by "asking around," like someone in the street needing directions. In the fall of 2008, with the help of the doctor and his sister, I met with two young Brothers, Ahmad Tawil and Hussein Maher, who were working in one of the group's low-cost food markets. They described themselves as Muslim men trying to help the needy in their everyday struggles. I asked whether they compared their work to that of global food movements that campaign for food welfare. The young Brothers liked my comparison. Ahmad looked down at my notebook, instructing, "Write that ours is Islam based." "Is this *activism*?" I asked, using the English word. Hussein responded teasingly in Arabic and English, "Why not, it makes us modern. But remember to write down 'Islam-based food activism.'" Smiling, Ahmad patted Hussein on the shoulder and said in a blend of Arabic and English, "Let it be 'Islam-based food activism [the] *ibn balad* way.'" Hence, in this chapter I use the terms "activism" and "activist," including the concept of *ibn balad*, to describe the Brotherhood's range of food provisions and outreach.

Ahmad and Hussein became the first in a long chain of Brothers who, over the years, have led me to different corners of Cairo in search of Islamic food schemes. This chapter uses ethnographic data gathered particularly during the revolution of 2011 and the following two years, after the ousting of the Mubarak regime. It draws on a core group of Brothers between the ages of twenty and forty who came from the same class backgrounds as the other men in this book. My Brotherhood interlocutors lived or came from the historic, popular quarter of inner Cairo and were, for the most part, students or educated professionals such as doctors, engineers, teachers, lawyers, and bureaucrats. They were highly motivated and accomplished, proud to be among the best and brightest students in their classes. It was also important to them for me to know that despite their family connections and urban mannerisms, their achievements come from God and devoted work. These men recounted their own beginnings as food activists and relayed stories about older generations of food activists. They included me on regular visits to poor households where they distributed food, showed me bakeries and grocery stores administrated or sponsored by the Brotherhood, and took me to their food market stalls, which were basically fruit and vegetable carts parked in lower-income neighborhoods. I was allowed to take photographs as long as I didn't identify the Brothers; otherwise, I watched and listened to their daily routine. I always carried a notebook openly and regularly wrote notes. Occasionally, when I was not writing, they worried that I was protecting them, assuring me that they had "nothing to hide."

In this chapter, I refer to how and why the youth branch of the Brotherhood started questioning why people had to struggle for food, and what the Brothers started to do about it. The why was the beginning of an analysis of the failure of food markets—that is, the absence of food in some people's everyday lives. The what was faith-based activism: religiously based ideas and actions expressed individually and collectively about personal and societal life, about being a Muslim, about being a Brother—in short, about being an activist in its totality and plurality of meanings—and about moral cosmologies, food, and action.

From the beginning, the Brotherhood insisted that active,

practical efforts to heal society were required for a good Islamic society (Lia 1998). The Brotherhood advocated social justice while criticizing greed, waste, and the lack of restraint (Munson 2001). The Brothers talked about the need to improve redistribution and the moral obligation to help those in need. These aims were religiously driven practices, and they invited questions regarding how individual activism intersects with everyday spiritual life in Egypt, as well as with broader economic and political concerns.

My conversations and observations attended to the particulars of individual Brothers as they engaged in morally driven practices. These particulars undermined attempts to generalize about the Brotherhood, Islam, or activism. There were evident activity patterns and economic philosophies among the Brothers, for instance, but they could not fully define Islam or typify the Brotherhood. Indeed, the ethnographic approach outlined in this chapter foregrounds the range of moral practices that surround economy and Islamic food activism. The moral economy is defined here as the capacity to forge relationships based on faith, practice, and moral order. To this end, many relationships organized around finding food for the deprived are seen as moral relations that go beyond Islamic doctrine. My argument is that theology and pragmatism are intertwined in food. Neither religious codification nor unorthodox practice completely defines outreach and activism. Hence, the emerging agency of the young Brothers is shown in their efforts to democratize food access in communities while also displaying their religious sensibilities. Religion, like economics and politics, involves morality, practice, controversy, and convention—notions not always classified as religious.

I suggest that the Muslim Brotherhood's food-justice activism was born of a politics of silence and exposure. As Carrie Rosefsky Wickham (2004, 233) argues in her ethnography of outreach among young Brotherhood members in the 1980s, "The social embeddedness of Islamic networks also permitted a certain amount of flexibility and experimentation, enabling graduates to 'try out' different levels and forms of participation without initiating a break from their social circles." In 2008 and during the uprising in 2011, I observed and listened to young Brothers increasingly challenge the authority of both the state and older members of the Brotherhood.

Although the ways in which young members recounted and engaged in activism produced a certain degree of normative behavior and sustained Islamic standards, their accounts and practices chipped away at established norms. Their challenge to the Brotherhood establishment may have related to activist currents that converged on the performance of particular practices. Although these human actions were inspired by Islamic values, they transcended and sometimes bypassed religious doctrine. I propose to call these morally directed, economically driven, and deeply paradoxical religious sentiments in food activism "Islamic food activism." Hence, Islamic food activism is a set of activist interventions embedded in Islamic religious beliefs and actions, and undertaken to promote food democracy. It enables young members of the Brotherhood to act out their religious faith in concrete practices promoting equitable food access and propagates a positive picture of their religion to Egyptian citizens.

With Islamic food activism, I introduce the activists' reconceptualization of faith as a set of interactions in process, examining how faith as devotion or space can lead to political action for social change. In what ways does piety drive the Brotherhood's food activism? Where is the social life of Islamic food activism?

FEEDING THE OTHERS

Two weeks before Egypt's first free parliamentary elections in November 2011, and a few days before the traditional Islamic rituals for the Feast of Sacrifice (Eid al-Adha), Muslim Brotherhood youth in Cairo gathered outside mosques in poor neighborhoods. They stood under a banner emblazoned with "Know Us, Join Us" and yelled out prices on discounted green beans, potatoes, onions, and other vegetables. Critics called it vote buying, yet another attempt by the Brotherhood to win over the hearts and souls of the poor (Tadros 2012). The distribution of bread and meat to the poor has been, throughout the Brotherhood's history in Egypt, among the most potent political efforts in its claim for legitimacy among ordinary Egyptians (Naguib 1996). In 2011, I observed as the Brotherhood responded to their critics by arguing in the media that food justice was a continuation of their outreach to all Egyptians.

Nancy J. Davis and Robert Robinson (2012, 47) claim, "The Brotherhood's work among professionals, students, and unemployed graduates was crucial in winning over those who became the most active and successful recruiters for the movement and in increasing its legitimacy with the broader public." Since its establishment in 1928, the Muslim Brotherhood has bypassed the state and established far-reaching networks that provide public service projects—mosques, clinics, schools, legal aid, day care centers, discount grocery stores, bread outlets, sports programs, and much more (see Burgat 2002; Davis and Robinson 2012; Zahid 2012).

While I do not go as far as François Burgat (2002), who suggests that the Muslim Brotherhood serves as the most legitimate and democratic expression of mass-based social activism in Egypt, my ethnography suggests that the youth branch's sense of political democracy, economic justice, moral obligation, and religious identity lends it a populist authenticity. It is worth noting that the Brotherhood was not the only youth movement demanding democracy in Egypt; the April 6 youth movement played a significant role in the protests that led to the occupation of Tahrir Square on January 25, 2011. But the youth branch of the Muslim Brotherhood, whether by legitimate or illegitimate means, has been the steadiest force in Egyptian civil society (see Zahid 2012).

Two striking features puzzled me during my research among Brotherhood food activists. First, they did not want to be categorized as mere members of a political social movement with close links to the headquarters, but rather as those who purposely reached out. The argument, related by a young activist, was that "the older generation is inward looking and only concerned with building the Brotherhood, while we are outward looking." He explained how members of the old guard communicated only among themselves, while the young branch interacted online with young people outside the Brotherhood.

Although my interlocutors felt affinities with the Brotherhood's Islamic guidelines, they were not prepared to let themselves be mobilized into actions in which they did not believe. I thus found a dynamic range of variations, beyond questions of religion, linked with other features of organization and identity. The young Brothers had protested several times before the popular revolution in 2011. They wanted a greater role for themselves, as individuals, in the Brotherhood (Davis and Robinson 2012; Tadros 2012). A young activist explained his personal wishes for independent mobilization outside constraints of headquarters:

> The old men have to develop an up-to-date approach to world realities. They act like fathers in old times. These times are past. We have faith just like them. We are also bound to God in a lasting relationship. But we use what God taught us proactively, since the world is changing around us. There are people out there who don't have food. I want to be out there helping them. I am inspired by Islam to do good. I combine my Muslim faith and my energy in mobilizing against food injustice and for food sovereignty. The old men in the Brotherhood are happy with the state of affairs. They don't understand that this is a mobilization for democratic control over food production and food distribution. I do what I do because I care about the last people in the food chain, those who are left out and come to the door.

This statement includes a number of interesting elements: personal aspirations established through food activism, the intensity of commitment to people who "come to the door," and the argument that Islamic activism, in varying degrees and ways, straddles the boundaries between orthodoxy and nonconformity, the traditional and the modern, the old and the young, and the local and the global. But the immediate point of the statement is to show that religion can be progressive. Complex religious clues lie just beneath the surface: rather than discuss difference and doctrine, this Brother talked about himself as committed to a morally driven economy, justice, and democracy.

The moral economy has particular significance in moments of upheaval, in which the imaginary and agency are likely to be intensified. The unfolding dramas of long breadlines made it possible to observe the Brothers during a period of economic disarray and food crisis. Although Brotherhood food activists acted "for the love of God," they were visible in the Egyptian social welfare landscape and thus seemingly demanded to be heard, both by Brotherhood elders and by society at large. By accepting the Brotherhood's offering of food safety nets, individuals became bound to reciprocate through some sort of commitment to the Brotherhood. For the Brothers, there is no incompatibility between Islam and the democratic structures of a compassionate society, commerce, and government.

When my interlocutors wanted to stress their claims for food justice, they referred to Qur'anic verses that speak of how this world is only transitory and how the hereafter is "better and more lasting." What they did in this life to help others would have consequences in the next. Accordingly, food activism and related economic activities were carried out among "our brothers and sisters" yet were clearly aimed "for God." Driven by faith, their aid "looks adversity right in the eye and deals with it," said Sherif Hassan, a young Brother with a degree in economics from the American University in Cairo.

Hassan always explained his actions with references to Qur'anic verses highlighting his argument about the links between Islamic economic activity and divine authority. He was one of my first interlocutors in 2008, and over the years he has talked to me about how religion urges all Muslims to honor the dignity of others and to distribute food in God's way. Underlying the notion of distributing food in God's way is the idea that all food belongs to God, who is "the decision maker." This goodness from God must be managed in accordance with God's sanctions by balancing the earthly with the heavenly, and the individual with the communal. As a human need, food presents a test of how one should live. Sherif talked about how people who have too much money were easily corrupted by plenty, and "plunged" into excess: "Islamic activity is about telling everybody that a Muslim's wealth is governed by communal obligations that stress the rights of the needy, poor, orphaned, and drifters." As a believing activist, Sherif is motivated by a desire to do more and to actively contribute to voluntary work, "like distributing food and collecting charity [in order] to be able to sell good-quality food at affordable prices."

For my interlocutors, social justice has primacy within their food-justice activism and within what they called "the Islamic and moral solution." Drawing on comparative studies on food riots, such as those in eighteenth-century England, E. P. Thompson (1991) argues that moral economy is not simply about regular access to food at a certain price and particular moment in history. Instead, food carries deep cultural as well as economic significance. Moreover, religion becomes equated with subjective states of faith, and ritual with symbolic action. If we take food and particular practices of everyday spirituality as contributing to people's needs and also to the young Brothers' identity and aspirations, then Islamic food activism may be analyzed as a practice that established connections between those receiving food and the Brothers providing food. Islamic food activism falls into this realm of societal relationships and questions, which inform adaptable faith-based processes, with all their potentialities and contradictions.

"FIELD OF STRUGGLE"

In *Life Within Limits: Well-being in a World of Want*, Michael D. Jackson (2011, ix) uses the term "field of struggle" to point to emotional and physical spaces that make life livable in a harsh and cruel world. I borrow "field of struggle" to think about faith-driven activities and spaces created by the economy of food. Jackson's interlocutors in Sierra Leone talked about not what they got out of life but how they should bear their loads. Jackson learned from his long conversations in the field that this thought could not be separated from relational obligations and the needs of others.

Jackson's work was helpful when I reflected on observations and conversations with young Brothers while they were engaging in food activism. But I go beyond that to suggest that, as this chapter's epigraph indicates, there is a relation between struggle and hope. For example, on a cold December day in 2011, I was sitting on a bench outside a subsidized bread outlet in a Cairo suburb with Karim Nasser, a member of the Muslim Brotherhood's youth movement. Karim, who was studying law, placed a pile of papers and books on the bench between us. The uppermost items caught my eye: writings on genetically modified foods, climate change, and food security, along with a book on the life of the Prophet Muhammad. We chatted about his Brotherhood activities over tea from the nearby coffee shop, running through issues such as whether Islam was the only solution to the growing poverty in Egypt, whether being a believer meant being a better person than a nonbeliever, whether religious activists do better than other kinds of activists in outreach, and whether people trust believers more than nonbelievers. People began to gather outside the bread kiosk to participate in our conversation. Many shared stories about rising food prices, indigestible bread, contaminated meat, the absence of basic foodstuffs, and hunger. A father of three told me that life had worsened after the revolution: "Jobs pay too little, and food costs too much. Where are the bread, dignity, and jus-

FIGURE 8. A meal is not a meal without bread, 2011.

tice?" In Egypt's first democratic parliamentary elections, in 2011, he voted for the Muslim Brotherhood, for a variety of reasons: "They understand how Egyptians struggle. They are not terrorists, like people think. They help for the love of God and give us some dignity back. And most of all they are not corrupt."

Not to lose their place in line, people, mostly men, moved closer to the outlet. Karim and I moved away. "Our faith drives us to do and be good," Karim said. "Our efforts are done with respect and humility. The objective is to facilitate the distribution of food for every Egyptian who needs it, without discrimination between women or men, Muslim or Christian." Smiling, he stroked his beard and said, "Just because we have beards doesn't make us evil."

We saw large wooden trays of round, earthy, flat layers of bread emerge. The crowd got loud; people pushed and shoved, trying to reach the small window where bread was being distributed. Desperate faces. It was a painful sight. A man with his hand on his young son's shoulder looked at my camera and implored, "Please don't take a picture. Let us keep some of our dignity." I put the camera away. Out of nowhere, young men with trimmed beards walked over. One walked into the store; the others stood outside and graciously greeted the shopkeeper. The crowd calmed down. Who were these young men? I asked. "Muslim Brotherhood food vigilantes," laughed the father with the son. According to Karim, they made irregular visits to neighborhoods that have suffered from clashes in bread queues. The Brothers, Karim said, were never involved in violence: "On the contrary, we come to calm down people." He described the visits as "food jihad." What he meant by that is worth reproducing at length:

> For us the Qur'an is the literal word of God, and it was revealed by the Prophet Muhammad and recorded by his companions as he recited it. This is our all-embracing approach to Islam, and it is universal. We share it with all other Muslims. It unifies us in our day-to-day struggle. For us, like all Muslims, to have faith comes with commandments and recommendations, and it shapes the way our lives will be lived and will end. The Qur'an is always in our mind. The Book is not only part of our culture, it also gives us emotional support for our jihad—our struggle for justice. Jihad means effort and not terror. Jihad means the struggle for the love of God. What you see today is a struggle [for the Brotherhood] to keep away food traders who bribe storekeepers into selling subsidized bread, which is then later sold in the streets at a higher price.

Karim and I ended up at the food kiosk because I had asked him whether he would point me to Brotherhood activities at public food outlets. He decided to show me what he described as an example of state food corruption, or, as he put it, "the immorality of state economics," whose activities routinely victimized the poor: "Whether you trade in arms or wheat, it's the same thing. The common people are the ones that feel most of the pain. We want to heal and give them hope." The totality of Islam, Karim explained, extended to all concerns of everyday life. Like many examples of Brotherhood charity work that I have studied for close to two decades, this one typifies the group's efforts to burrow into the community through faith and outreach. The statement of the father of three in the breadline that the Muslim Brothers were "not terrorists, like people think" dispels fears of the Brotherhood's sectarianism by describing how they "watch over" communities. Davis and Robinson (2012, 59) show how this "watching over" goes back to el-Banna's vision: "It's the religious duty of every Muslim to work towards the transformation of society. Words alone were not enough to re-Islamize Egyptian society; action was needed."

Especially during my time in Tahrir Square in 2011 and during the first hundred days of the country's Islamist regime, I noticed that although young members' desire for community outreach continued, they critically questioned older Brothers. Young Brothers became assertive and demanded that the society and its decision-making channels become more dynamic than previously. Young members were involved in civil society, and as in the above case from the bread outlet, they operated in poor neighborhoods and were able to represent themselves and their faith for "the best possible reasons," as Karim said. The Brothers' moral obligation, he explained, was "to show solidarity and to provide people with the possibility of a decent meal and try to prevent food corruption." These areas were among those the Brothers considered essential: "Food, health, and education are the only ways to heal the Egyptian sense of dignity and calm down society." How easy would that be? I asked. Karim replied: "Easy. We mobilize or join other young people in their protests. The difference between us and the other protesters is that we do it through the route of Islam and the struggle for justice—jihad. True Islam is what you saw today on your visit."

My visit drew attention to how, in the context of breadlines, Islamic activism mobilized and constructed collective piety that inspired the Brothers' solidarity with people's grievances. Distributing bread was a public demonstration of the Brotherhood's extension of "true Islam." The meaning and applicability of food jihad, for Karim, was a direct response to the political order, economic hardship, and social life.

Mikhail Bakhtin (1981) wrote something to the effect that hell is the absolute lack of being heard. Karim, like the other Brothers, said that they not only hear but also see and "show solidarity" with the faces of humiliated Egyptians standing in endless breadlines. The difficulties this activism presented were not confined to matters of grasping the struggles of those who lived "ordinary sufferings" (Bourdieu et al. 1999), but also addressed the ways in which the Brothers drove relentless food jihad so as to reorder the world through actions that involved food, which, I argue, required human anticipation and hope.

Hope as a key component in healing people's grievances featured strongly in my conversation with Karim and other young Brothers. Shortly after my visit to the bread outlet, I interviewed a young Brother who complained about how corrupt economic practices destroy traditional Egyptian family values, and the subject of "broken human spirits" came up. I asked him about the causes of broken spirits, and he listed several, including "a spiritually broken and offended body."

The people in the breadlines, at the mercy of the rising prices of grain and the scarcity of bread, manifested the absolute and arbitrary nature of crude economics on the human body. The body is the primary site on which the imprint of economics can be seen and human spirit damaged. Whether in the context of orderly eating or disorderly breadlines, the body is the means by which the veracities of the food economy are expressed and demonstrated. Whether the body is well nourished or hungry, it ultimately "bears witness" (Fassin 2012) to political power and food justice.

In response to my question on whether Islam—in the sense of having sufficient faith—was enough to bring about change, one of my interlocutors, who regularly did volunteer work at a low-cost grocery store, responded by saying simply, "Of course." When I questioned him further, he replied matter-of-factly: "We are guided by conscience. It is not always easy to do the right thing. But with a pure conscience, I am able to balance between the here and now and the hereafter, when God will judge my deeds." Religion and faith fostered the capacity and potentiality for compassion and possibility to bring about change. Through their efforts for justice, the Brothers aimed for feelings of moral solidarity that could enable community and individual agency. This form of activism and aspiration for change resided in a complex mix of their being themselves, cultivating relationships with others, and imagining a new order. I expand elsewhere on this idea of human agency as human potential (Naguib 2010) and return to it in this chapter. It is interesting to note how the Brothers' aspirational food ideas began to break toward new potential and hope. Their attempts to reestablish links between Islamic values and society demonstrated how they saw themselves in relation to society and how they made sense of their lives and the lives of those for whom they provided. This link between aspiration and agency served as a way to reconstruct hopeful futures for themselves and society (Appadurai 2007).

BREAD AND PRAYERS

Bread can signal prosperity, distress, anxiety, and social and political mobilization. Bread, a remarkable commodity, represents both substance and symbol. It provides nourishment and serves as a key mode of communication having spiritual, cultural, social, political, and economic inflections. Bread is one of the key actors in Egyptian social, political, and economic life. This was powerfully displayed during the 2011 revolution, when women held up pieces of bread and men made helmets from bread. The slogan was "Bread, Dignity, and Social Justice." Bread has a significant influence on private and public relationships, bringing about positive memories of meals and equally strong emotions about deprivation.

Bread forges complicated links between people and faith, justice and injustice, hope and anguish, whole and part, producer and consumer, seller and buyer, and most of all, as one baker said, "loyalty and duty."

Eating bread is one of the most satisfying acts involving the human senses: the mouth-watering smell of freshly baked bread, its warmth in the hand, and its fulfilling taste. "Remember," Mustafa told me, "the word for bread in Egyptian Arabic is *aish*—life." Mustafa was an engineer and food activist who visited bakeries to ensure that they were not mixing coarse government-provided flour with dirt and sawdust when producing the traditional dark flat bread sold at a set price. As a small schoolchild, he learned that Egypt was the breadbasket of the Roman Empire. Mustafa referred to what he read in the newspapers: "Bread is strategic. Egypt is the world's largest importer of wheat, and Egyptians eat the most bread in the world." After calculating his household expenses, Mustafa told me that food prices had risen "17 percent in just one year." This increase had enormous implications for the country: "In a nation where one in five lives on an income of less than $1 per day, subsidized bread is for millions of Egyptians the only calorie intake."

Mustafa went on to explain, "The challenge is that the amount of money that is possible to make from this inferior flour would make anybody accept a bribe." Governmental bakeries receive flour from the government to produce subsidized bread. Although bakers receive a salary from the government, the problem of corruption starts when "the baker puts aside the flour and sells it on the black market for a larger profit." Mustafa explained that there were governmental inspectors whose job was to prevent this. These inspectors received a governmental salary of about $50 a month. If they certified that after three months the baker had faithfully used the flour to bake bread, the baker got a refund of about one dollar for every bag of flour he purchased.

Mustafa said that a baker who went through forty sacks of flour a day over the three-month period got back a decent sum:

[Which] he can easily share with the same underpaid inspector who confirms that the baker has not broken any rules. Poverty pushes people to compromise. The inspector is a man who gets fifty American dollars. Say he wants to feed his children three times a day, send them to the government school. Of course going to any government school, they will need afternoon tutoring. And say this inspector wants to take his wife out for a simple meal of Egyptian street food. Perhaps even take the kids along. What if this man wants to surprise his wife with half a kilo of good meat for Friday lunch? Maybe he even desires to buy her a new dress, shoes, or anything to make her happy? He can't. But he wants to—very much.

I asked Mustafa whether food inspectors took bribes, and he replied, "Yes, they do." Mustafa's account shows the gray zones generated by wheat and bread subsidies. This case illustrates the divisive and repressive connection between politics and economy that the Brotherhood activists seek to eradicate.

GOD PROVIDES

Osman Galal was a young, sophisticated, articulate, and French-speaking Brother. His membership in the Brotherhood went against his family's wishes. At his home in an upscale neighborhood, we talked about the possible reasons for the popularity of the Brothers among Egyptian men of different social backgrounds.

Osman attributed the group's success to its "openness and respect for the diversity of Egyptian society." It was linked, he said, with the ways the Brotherhood first gained prospective members' sympathy and then recruited them. He described how the Brotherhood created a pool of new members who were invited, "but never forced to join meetings or campaigns." Instead, the Brothers connected with people's ordinary lives: "When people see that we care, they join the Brotherhood. We move easily from our personal, everyday life to activism." Their outreach infrastructure was based on networking in communities and on building communal locations like mosques, clinics, schools, food outlets, women's vocational training centers, and soccer fields, which allowed them to fulfill their promises of social and economic assistance.

An active Brotherhood presence in people's everyday lives lends material legitimacy to its message that Islam is the true path to democratic development. Osman explained, "Our message is not just a set of empty ideas debated by leaders you only see on TV; our message of faith is linked to practical activities that attend to people's real concerns—like food on the table." Key to their success, Osman said, was that their "ideas are tied directly to action" in concrete and identifiable ways. He elaborated: "For example, when we say Islam is the solution, we don't mean, let's go kill people. We mean, let's build a mosque, let's provide shelter for orphans, kindergartens, clinics, and let's make sure people get their bread and not grimy bread. We demand good bread for all."

As an Islamic food activist, Osman felt a particular sense of satisfaction that allowed him to imagine a better future for himself and others. His reasoning showed how the relationship between ideas and the structure of the group was key to overcoming the universal problem of uneven degrees of commitment and beliefs.

HEART AND SOUL

Despite the obvious, inevitable, and strong links between the young Brothers and Islamic guidelines, their food activism demonstrated the need to be analytically attentive to specific forms of religious and social entanglements. The Islamic food activists in this chapter were not part of a fanatical opposition movement. Their tracts, efforts, and conversations revealed actions concerned with contemporary economic issues, such as food supply and food corruption. Their food activism was linked with Islam in such a way that each movement was strengthened and made more resilient and attractive to Egyptians from different backgrounds. One Brother described his obligation to heal people's food grievances as "food for the soul." Their efforts and slogans, rooted in Islamic concepts and representations, were tied to everyday events and ordinary Egyptian household economies. Therefore, the group was easily accessible to those who relied on its support, which strengthened the potential for recruitment.

In writing this chapter, I wanted to do more than simply bring together conversations with Islamic activists and highlight their personal relationships with piety and food justice. Their efforts, told here with an emphasis on bread and breadlines, promoted an exploration of generational gaps within Islamic movements, particularly of those emerging from young men demanding fresh forms of political, economic, and social engagement. The material experience of bread— its fundamentality to Egyptian households and its moral basis for piety and society—was a crucial part of the Brothers' driving force and activism. Their physical engagement with supplying bread to the people, the regular nonviolent battles against the corruption of flour, and the spectacle of their peaceful actions illustrated how and why individuals modified, re-created, and aimed to engage in practices that could lead to social change.

Activism involves a shifting praxis in the realms of everyday religious life and social action. While Islamic food activism involves giving recognition, hope, and significance to people's everyday misfortunes, my ethnographic material shows that religion as the principal driving force for activism is not totalizing, nor are its outcomes easily predictable. This chapter provides an interpretation of how young members of the Brotherhood drove institutional outreach and infused community with Islam through their brand of faith-based activism. It attempts to understand what particular actions involving Islam and food mean and how they link religion, pragmatism, and activism.

CHAPTER 3

SUCH IS THE LIFE OF MEN

Such is the life of a man. Moments of joy, obliterated by
unforgettable sorrow. There's no need to tell the children that.
MARCEL PAGNOL, *LE CHÂTEAU DE MA MÈRE*

THE EPIGRAPH TO THIS CHAPTER comes from a novel that
tells the poignant story of the author's family as seen from a
child's point of view. Pagnol recounts banquets and bouquets,
freshly baked breads, an abundance of fresh thyme, and jars
of olive oil arranged neatly in the village market. There are
family feasts, happy occasions, and warm smiles. Pagnol
wrote about what he knew best: life in the south of France,
tight-knit families bound by a life of loyalty, conviviality,
and decency. Prompted by Pagnol's passionate recollections
and love for his family (and my own affection for his stories),
I want to remember the many agreeable meals I shared with
my interlocutors and the many wonderful stories they re-
called from their youths.

   Some of the most agreeable moments I have experienced
in my three decades as an anthropologist in the Middle East
have been while sharing meals with men, women, and children who graciously accommodated and fed me. During the
past ten years, my fieldwork has been concerned mostly
with wars and revolutions—global moments that shape human life. I have also concentrated on women's everyday
concerns, activities, struggles, and accomplishments dur-

ing these times of rupture. Some of the most humane insights into individual stories came while preparing, eating, and talking about food. While the men walked in and out of the kitchen, commented on the fragrance of food, and participated in conversations around the dinner table, I focused on what women were saying in order to gather information about ingredients, recipes, and dishes. My research argued that family stories and metaphors provide a key to understanding the emotive power of how women experience their enduring attachments to people and places. While women, and sometimes children, are present in this chapter, most of it is given over to men's nostalgic longings. My point of departure is Mustafa Hashim, whom we met in chapter 1, and a group of men who meet in a bakery in Cairo.

Let me open by retrieving Mary Douglas's (1974) now-classic anthropological formulation in "Deciphering a Meal." Douglas's work is known for its structuralist analysis of the meal as made up of A + 2B (one meat and two vegetables), and the many algebraic elaborations of this basic formula, but also concerns the relations between meals. She sees these relations as a system of repeated analogies. Each meal, to be a meal, must recall the basic structure of other meals. I extend this idea and include the ability of a meal to recall private lives that become memorable as sensory, as well as social, experiences.

Each man I interviewed had a story about a specific food and a particular meal, and each woman talked about her husband's struggles to be a good family man. These men told stories about how they were torn between traditional and modern worlds. Tearing bread represented many things. When Mustafa Hashim carefully picked a warm round loaf of bread from the wooden shake and tore a piece for me to touch and taste, it spurred personal memories and inspired concentration. It was also the first exchange I had with men about food—its texture, taste, fragrance, and appearance. In a particularly expressive example, Mustafa's baker pulled out a metal tray, put three lumps of sugar in each of three glasses,

FIGURE 9. Sweet tea, 2004.

and poured strong tea into each glass. Then he went to a tray
with freshly baked bread and asked one of his young appren-
tices to pull out chairs. He placed the tray on the table and
offered me a loaf of burning-hot bread, saying, "Now, *ya doctora*, you see a genuine man's gathering."

But I am getting ahead of myself. I want to return to recollections. A good way to do this is to recall the essence of re-
peating stories. In his beautiful book *Wisdom Sits in Places*,
Keith Basso (1996, 37) recalls Clyde Kluckhohn's statement
made during a lecture at Harvard University in 1960: "The
most interesting claims people make are those they make
about themselves. Cultural anthropologists should keep this
in mind, especially when they are doing fieldwork." Stories
have a way of shaping what we remember. Hence, my attempt with close narratives is to show that when men talk
about food, they are in fact retelling and recalling the sweet-
est and severest moments in their lives. Olivia Harris (1996)
poses central questions about what it means for people to go

through change. She asks us to look closely at temporalities of not only change but also tradition. Here are two concepts that "indicate notions of order, of legitimacy, and above all of continuity" (Harris 1996, 2). What Harris refers to as temporalities, which I borrow to talk about masculine nurturing, cannot be understood if we do not take Kluckhohn's advice to heart. People's claims can be thick or thin.

REAL MEN EAT FAT

Mustafa Hashim once teased me about my research, saying that he did his own "food and men" research and concluded that there was one ingredient that signified Egyptian cooking: "*samna baladi*, with no doubt": "It's the flavor of Egyptian cooking. An ingredient an Egyptian man cannot live without." His wife, Hoda, had, after years of marriage, learned to add the right amount of *samna*, meaning, according to Mustafa, "[It is] just the way I like it. You know, every home has a way of cooking. Her father is used to less *samna* than I."

Mustafa liked to repeat that he was an ordinary Egyptian man who liked to eat ordinary Egyptian food. He had this to say about his wife's early cooking:

You know, the madam is an educated lady. She reads and likes to watch the scientific programs on TV. Since I drive all day, I don't like her to work, she spends her time reading and watching TV. So one Friday I decide to stay at home. I go to the kitchen and there she is washing a pigeon. I have never seen my mother do this. Why? Because she wants to wash away excess fat. Why? And then she shows me a bottle of olive oil. She was going to start making rice with olive oil. I have to tell you, *ya doctora*, I got very angry and I raised my voice for the first time in our fifteen-year marriage. I did not want to see olive oil in the cooking. She can pour it on the squash and add lemons.

Then he looked at my notebook and said, "*Ya doctora*, this is important for your project. An Egyptian man wants tasty food. *Samna* is crucial."

Samna baladi is clarified butter and the most favored cooking fat. Food is not the same without it, according to Mustafa. His story began with an account of his childhood, when his mother would get her tins of *samna baladi* from her family in the Saaid (Upper Egypt):

> I remember as a boy when my mother would take me along to visit her family. I have seen them make *samna*. It's something they do in spring. First, butter is made from buffalo milk. Then they melt it over boiling water. It is then clarified by straining it through very thin, damp, gauze-like cloth. All the impurities that make butter burn and get black are reduced with this process. So you get fat with no water. *Samna baladi* has all the goodness that gets washed out with ordinary butter. And also, just a little has the same effect as a much larger quantity of butter. Except for the taste. *Samna baladi* is strong; the concentrated fat makes the food tasty. Every year my grandmothers and aunts would send up with a relative or friend a couple of tins of *samna baladi* for all of us. You know it can stay for years without getting bad.

In all the years I have known Mustafa, I had rarely seen him frown and speak so seriously. He went on, speaking slower than usual, to explain that *samna baladi* has great health benefits:

> Everyone is very concerned about eating organic food. Well, *samna baladi* is purely organic, excuse the expression. The buffalo graze on *barseem* (clover-like grass). This makes good fat. Personally, I think it has antistress benefits. You know, for a workingman like me, just the fragrance calms me down. It brings back memories. Friday lunch with my mother's cooking is sacred to me. You know, I climb the

stairs to her apartment, and the fragrance catches me. I see
my whole childhood in front of me. The stuff they produce
in the factories is not *samna*. They should not be calling
it *samna*. It does not have the same strong fragrance that
makes your mouth water.

A couple of weeks after this conversation, I admitted to
Mustafa that I agreed with his wife's health concern that
samna is high in cholesterol and not good for the heart, that
perhaps he should alternate between olive oil and *samna*, and
that, personally, I always cook my rice with olive oil. Mustafa announced: "You have to taste my mother's rice." Indeed, Mustafa discussed the "story of rice" with his mother
and sisters. It was decided also that I needed cooking lessons.
I was thereby invited to his mother's home for Friday lunch.
It was an invitation to cook with *samna baladi*. A few days
before, Mustafa called to tell me that his mother wanted me
to come early: "She wants to teach you to cook Egyptian
style."

A MAN'S FRIDAY LUNCH

In Egyptian households, the preparation of rice is shrouded
in ritual secretiveness. It is an extremely simple dish cooked
in a large number of ways. Each family cherishes a particular method and is skeptical of all others. When Um Mustafa first came to Cairo as a young girl, she worked for a "fine
family." She was very lucky, since the lady of the house was
"a real lady who knew God." What is more, "she was kind
and the best cook." She insisted that Zeinab (Um Mustafa)
needed to learn to cook and "that learning to cook *afrangi*
(modern) food will serve me later in life." It did. When the
family moved to Canada, Um Mustafa (she was married then)
went to cook for a family of professors twice a week. They
had kept in touch and talked at least once a month. "The
lady of the house used to stay home on the days I cooked, [in
order] to learn. I would give her little tasks to do like peel the

squash, cut the garlic, rub the chicken in flour. Prepackaged rice was not allowed into the house when I was there. The lady learned to cook rice my way."

Now Um Mustafa, with the help of money from her first employer, a small pension from "the professors," and assistance from her sons, could stay at home, and a young girl "from our place" helped her with the housework. With great pleasure and a growing appetite, I watched as the sisters filled chickens with meat and pine nuts, rolled vine leaves, and filled pastries with mashed dates.

Rice is stored in burlap sacks. I was assigned the task of picking out the stones, straws, and loose fibers. Spotting prepackaged rice on a shelf, I suspected that Um Mustafa had instead decided to give me a thorough education in preparing and cooking rice from scratch. Mustafa's older sister came over, poured the cleaned rice into a plastic bowl, and told me that it was time to wash the rice, one of many times before cooking: "Wash and drain the rice. Let the rice dry out. Not too dry, but it must stop dripping water." Um Mustafa called out to her son: "Now it's time to cook the rice. The *doctora* will make it." Mustafa frowned, and his wife teased him about his skepticism. I assured him that his mother, sisters, and Fatma (the help) would supervise every step and make sure I did not reach for the olive oil. He smiled carefully: "Mama, watch out for Hoda and the *doctora*. I don't want this *afrangi* rice of the *doctora* and Hoda." Hoda, feigning offense, said, "You think it's right, *ya* Um Mustafa, that he talks to the *doctora* like this?" Turning to Mustafa, she admonished, "We will have words together when we get home today, *ya Si Mustafa* [Master Mustafa]."

His mother took out a ten-liter can of *samna baladi*. She scooped a few spoonfuls of *samna* into a saucepan, threw in the rice, and fried it gently "until . . . each rice grain [was] soaked with *samna*." Then she commanded, "Now give me the water and salt." She added water and salt, turned up the gas fire, and brought it to a strong boil "just for a couple of minutes." She then turned down the fire, covered the pot tightly with the lid, and placed an iron weight on top. The smell of cooking rice wafted out to the rest of the family in the sitting room.

Um Mustafa told me to lift the lid. The rice was tender with little holes on the surface. She lifted the rice and turned it perfectly onto a large platter. She strode into the dining room holding the steaming hot rice. The strong and distinct smell of rice fried and cooked in *samna* filled the room. Silence followed as everyone was served, a pause during which everyone seemed lost in his or her own thoughts. Compliments to Um Mustafa: bless the hands that prepared this meal! "It's the *doctora*," she teased. The conversation turned to everyday gossip. I looked across the table at Mustafa. He was quietly eating his food with a smile on his face. Like all my interlocutors, he was a courteous man who answered my questions about men and food with patience and a smile. But I had never seen him as outright content as he was there eating his mother's rice and meat stew with a spoon and a piece of bread.

The rice and the meat stew filled the house with the smells that generated conversations about past great and small occasions, family habits, friends, and the week's goings and comings, always accompanied by funny statements. When I look at the notes from my regular lunches at Um Mustafa's home and compare them with notes from my previous work on food and memory, it strikes me how the tastes and smells of food offer daily confirmation of what people carry with them and to what they keep returning. As Mustafa put it, "When I think of mama's cooking, my mouth waters."

THE BAKER AND HIS MEN

I mentioned to a baker in Cairo that I wanted to write something about men and food and that I was thinking of concentrating on bread. When I asked him whether he thought the bakery would be a good place to speak with people, he shrugged and replied, "Why not? It's normal." I asked him whether he thought that men would like to talk to me in the bakery. He sighed and said:

> Where else do you want to talk to them? Men are in the coffeehouse or the bakery. The coffeehouse is no place for a lady. The bakery is OK. People know you here. They are used to you. You can also combine baking and drinking tea. Ask a man about his piece of bread and he will not stop telling you stories—tea, and he will go on forever. Some of the stories might even be true. Yes, it's a good idea. Why not begin with me?

This exchange occurred in 2007. Since then, I have tracked the bakery men's sensory memories of taste, nostalgia for past periods of Cairo life as expressed in baking and bread, and what Sutton (2008, 163) calls "prospective memories," which he defines as "the active planning in the present for future memories."

I returned to visit Omar Farouk, the baker, during the uprisings in Cairo in 2011. The bakery was just down an alley, behind the city of the dead, where the poor live scattered amid forgotten graves. Here Omar baked bread. He worked from six o'clock in the morning until eight o'clock at night, earning less than $90 a month to pay the rent and raise his grandchildren. It has been this way for twenty years: his hands, quick as sparrows, feeding flat dough into an oven. About thirty people—mothers, fathers, children—waited for government-subsidized loaves. They laughed, worried, argued, and pressed their faces up to the metal bars, peering in and wondering what was taking Omar so long to bake another batch. Reflected Omar, "There used to be no bars between the baker and the people. Before, people were close and food had more blessing. The Egyptian oven was open. Beautiful. The fragrance of bread was everywhere. Fathers passed by on their way home to buy bread. Now, look, it's women. Where are the men?"

A girl with a silver tray slipped through a metal door,

FIGURE 10. A baker, 2010.

where more children waited with trays and wooden racks on which to stack the puffy hot bread emerging straight from Omar's oven. They balanced the trays on their heads to make deliveries, passing the stonecutter and the imam. Sunlight poured through a hole in the bakery's roof. Omar, standing barefoot in spilled flour, urged the children to hurry and stack the bread.

Once the bread arrived outside, the scent lingered. One of the men in the line called out to me, "Is there anything more precious than the scent of bread? We see it and smell it and relax. Life is hard. Life tries one's patience, tests our limits, and sometimes pushes us beyond it. The world was a happier place before. Here, it's old days."

Bread is more than sustenance in Egypt. It is a bond between people and state, a centuries-old promise that whatever else fails, there will always be bread. "Bread is like the soul to us," said Tarek, the bakery's manager. "It's the cheapest, most filling part of any meal. The government wanted to raise the price on the bread we bake. They said the price would go up but so would the quality. But they wouldn't increase quality. People went crazy. They didn't raise the price. Bread is a promise."

Eid, a bakery employee, took a break from kneading dough. When I first interviewed Eid about bread, he pointed to the camera hanging from my wrist, the video camera around my neck, the pen clipped onto my shirt, and the notebook in my blazer pocket: "Tell me, *ya doctora*, have you come on an expedition to observe a simple oven?" Not waiting for an answer, he continued: "There is more to the oven than just writing down notes or taking a film of one kilogram of flour and a bunch of tired men sitting around. There is taste and smell—tell me, *ya doctora*, how will you film and write about that?" I mumbled something absurd about putting it all in the context of Egyptian men and food, but Eid was not listening. Instead, he started telling me his story: he was thirty-four years old with wheat dust in his thinning hair. "I have a degree from university: Arabic literature," he said.

I do some teaching in the school. But that is nothing. Sometimes they forget to pay me. So I come here and make 20 pounds [$3.45] a day to cover my daily cigarettes. There's only one thing I really want in this life, to marry a woman. A woman I take good care of. And children. Then I can do like my father. Come home for lunch with a kilogram of oranges, strawberries, or a watermelon. I think of how it was when I was growing up. My father found the woman of his dreams on a full stomach—my mother.

His parents' favorite pastime was food shopping: "They memorized the prices of food from day to day, and they talked incessantly about food—what they were going to eat for lunch, for supper. And when they were eating, they were talking about what they would eat tomorrow. That generation had a good life in Egypt. They were passionate about food." He looked away.

"I've got seven kids," said Ahmed, another employee, his silver tooth glinting. "I have my two sons working here with me for extra income. I just want to live like a normal man, but now I can only put meat on the table once a year. But thank God I still come home with warm bread." Ahmed grew up in this neighborhood at a time when the desert rimmed closer to the city's heart and the banks of the Nile were not so crowded. Although Cairo is a big city now, it is familiar to him, like an extended family with stories to share. He knows the faces of his family waiting for bread: "We have stories together. You know, bread makes it easy to talk. Even better when you add a glass of tea." He went to boil water for tea.

Salheen, a heavyset assistant baker in a gray sweat suit with a mustache in need of tending, walked from Omar's oven toward the metal door. Faces from the outside pressed in. People wanted bread. "It's coming," he said. But the fifty sacks of flour the government delivered every day had not arrived. Protests were delaying the flow of everyday life. We could see burning buildings on the horizon.

"They have one worry: the bread on their table," said Omar Farouk:

> They don't care about politics. All they know is that they have to line up here every day. Like our fathers and forefathers did. It's our way of life. And between you and me—we men love it. You know, holding warm bread and walking home to the family. No matter what you have on the table, it's not complete without bread. It's a nice picture.

Omar sat down next to Eid and put an arm around the young man's shoulders; quietly, he told him that they are all lucky to have a job—and not just any job. There was something soothing about bread—the flour, the dough, and the oven. The other men nodded in silence; Eid nodded and said, "*Amin.*"

Fouad drove a taxi and was a close friend of Omar and the other men in the bakery. I first met him in 2008 when he stopped by a bakery where I was working on a study of bread and historical consciousness (Naguib 2009). At the time, he was in his late thirties, married, with four small children. Several times a week, Fouad would end up in the bakery at the end of the day, chatting and drinking tea. He was always good fun. He liked to joke, impersonating his customers and people he saw in the streets of Cairo. Since then, his life had changed dramatically:

> I can't go out with my wife and children. She has stopped looking at things, but children are children. They look at things. I can't get it for them. My father would get my mother and us children whatever we wanted. He was such a man who would take his wife—my dear mother—out shopping and tell her, "Pick what you want." He would tell the person behind the counter to give her what she pointed to and he would pay for it. He was a taxi driver. I grew up in a nice apartment. Not big; we are not those sorts of people. But it was a real apartment. What have I given my family? A hole in an unfinished building. With my salary, I can't cover food expenses. This is not the way things should be.

MOUTHWATERING RECOLLECTIONS

We look at the past and at moments in the past in different ways. For some, the past is "another country" (Lowenthal 1985), and we try to reconstruct it from traces left behind. Tastes and smells of food are traces that re-create and confirm what we carry with us and what we keep returning to. This chapter sketches cultural continuity among a group of men in Cairo in an attempt to understand how not only remembered foods such as *samna* or bread but also my interlocutor's mouthwatering visions of particular foods offer an unusual view of Egyptian men's—indeed, Arab men's—sentimentality and moments of human tenderness.

Links between food and sentimentality have produced some intriguing findings, such as descriptions of the preparations of specific dishes and the nostalgic performances of serving them in certain societies and not others. Food may well be such an item or place for memory rehearsals in certain societies and not others. In *The Architecture of Memory*, Joelle Bahloul (1996) outlines sites of food memories. Her ethnographic work is part of a larger literature on food, ruptures, life crises, and memory. Another scholar, Ulf Hannerz (1996, 27), offers a brilliantly suggestive anecdote about the first thing a Swedish couple did after a trip to Borneo: they drank a glass of cold milk at their kitchen table—"Home is where that glass of cold milk is." Sutton's book *Remembrance of Repasts: An Anthropology of Food and Memory* (2001) is devoted to how food constructs memory. Sutton's goal is to use food to explore questions of how memory works and to use "memory to energize studies of 'food past' by explicitly adding the question of historical consciousness to work that looks at food" (15). Turning to classic literature, we find the evocative *"petites madeleines"* that threw Proust back into a "remembrance of the past." In Hasia R. Diner's *Hungering for America: Italian, Irish, and Jewish Foodways in the Age of Migration* (2002), we learn how other sweet "agent[s] of memory" (8) shape ethnic identity and a sense of community.

As indicated above, scholars have long called attention to and elaborated on the fact that for humans, "eating is never a 'purely biological' activity" but rather one of many areas in which we invest "a basic activity with social meaning[s]" that are "symbolic," are "communicated symbolically," and "also have histories" (Mintz 1996, 7). Individual and collective memory are profoundly and densely embedded in, enacted through, and communicated symbolically through the many forms of engagement with food. An abundance of literature foregrounds and elaborates on the enduring and affecting qualities of early personal memories connected with food—"preserved in our bodily senses long after the intelligence has lost sight of them"; ironically, the senses most directly involved with eating—taste and smell—are seen simultaneously as "our most delicate and seemingly fragile senses" and as "the most persevering and zealous keepers of our past experiences" (Gilroy 1987, 100–101).

Many others highlight the operations of collective memory in great detail in connection with food. The "commemorative" function of food is elaborated extensively in a wide range of fields and writings, both in the act of consumption, which allows individuals to "partake each day" of the collective past, and in the preparation and cooking of food, which have "long roots" constituting "the repository of . . . the accumulated wisdom of our ancestors" (Barthes 1979, 170). A resurgence of scholarship on the relationship between food and many aspects of human experience has taken up, with renewed interest, the role of food in the social, religious, and cultural lives of people and the ways in which food consumption and preparation, and the diffusion of knowledge about food, have figured in individuals' self-concepts; their affiliations and identifications with home, homeland, and a range of social groupings; and the incorporation of these earliest and most persistently retained sense memories into the creation and structuring of collective memory and cultural identity.[1]

Fouad's anxieties indicate some of the subtle and complex interconnections among everyday forms of food provision in the present, memories of the past, and the wider political and economic contexts to which men must respond in order to fulfill their obligations. In focusing on the place of food in men's lives and memory, this book makes an argument about

1. It is beyond the scope of this book to address or even refer in passing to the voluminous and growing bibliography of writings on food and memory (individual and collective). For further reading, the following list of works can provide a starting point: Goody 1982; Kanafani 1983; Vaughan 1987; Stoller 1989; Scheper-Hughes 1992; Mennell et al. 1992; Kirshenblatt-Gimblett 1999; Tannahill 1988; Kugelmass 1990; Charsley 1992; Feeley-Harnik 1994; Mintz 1996; Counihan 1999; Zubaida and Tapper 2000; Sutton 1998, 2001; Korsmeyer 2005.

the complicated, endless, and shared relationships between the social and the personal and about the centrality of memory, discursively framed by men's accounts about being men.

Among my interlocutors, the past is imagined as a time when men easily brought food home and women had all the ingredients they needed in order to feed their men and children. Memories can be deeply social and gendered, since they are shaped by our interactions with the humans, objects, and locations that involve us in society, without necessarily needing to be widely shared. Maurice Halbwachs (1980) is in a sense right in claiming that all memory is social (no memory is, then, asocial). But we can also say that all memory is personal: organized by individuals moving along their particular trajectories and through their social landscapes.

This is the point made by neuroscientists who claim that memory continues to be crafted throughout life (Greenfield 2000, 1). A scholar of the brain's "plasticity," Susan Greenfield describes how, as the brain matures and becomes more complex, it draws more on personal experience and less on instinct. These personalized connections, which each person makes based on prior experiences, are found within small neuron networks. Greenfield's argument is that the mind is the personalization of the brain (14). So experience, in essence, is a personal endeavor, as is our ability to remember (and to forget). Both memory and forgetting are active processes; no matter how close we are to people in our lives, our experiences are exclusive and so are our emotional responses. The same can be said for culture, as anthropologists have been arguing for some time now (Garro 2000; M. Rosaldo 1980; R. Rosaldo 1993). This exclusiveness of experience and response also suggests a need to revisit Pierre Nora's (1996) well-known discussion of *milieux de mémoire* (environments of memory) and *lieux de mémoire* (spaces or sites of memory).

Omar's bakery shows how, in contemporary Egypt, even a casual visitor can see the importance of bakeries and bread in daily life and discourse. Food markets and bakeries are regarded as important places of human interaction—perhaps not surprisingly, in a society where particular foods, like bread, are heavily regulated and state subsidized. Bread is as much about moral economy as it is about moral thoughts. As a place that reaches deeply into other cultural spheres, Omar's bakery is a matrix and a method for understanding men's conception of being men, their notions of aesthetics, and the workings of memory. The bakery is both a place for recalling the past, "when things were good," and a participant in the creation and re-creation of such nostalgia. Recollections belong to forms of memory that are culturally shaped by the place they occupy in peoples' lives. It is trivial but significant; it is what, as Sutton (2001) suggests, makes Paul Connerton's *How Societies Remember* (1989) such a powerful reference for anthropologists doing work on sites of memory.

Bakery stories driven by taste, memory, and real life communicate reality in a basic way about everyday life and everyday places. Keith Basso (1996, xiii) points out that we tend not to think too much about the "sense of place":

> We tend not to think [that the sense of place is complex],
> mainly because our attachments to places, like the ease with
> which we usually sustain them, are unthinkingly taken
> for granted. As normally experienced, sense of place quite
> simply *is*, as natural and straightforward as our fondness
> for certain colors and culinary tastes, and the thought that
> it might be complicated, or even very interesting, seldom
> crosses our minds.

In *Remembrance of Repasts*, Sutton (2001, 89) directly addresses the presence of powerful stimuli, smells that can "be recognized over a distance of many years": "The fact that taste and smell have a much greater association with episodic than semantic memory, with the symbolic rather than the linguistic, and with recognition rather than recall, helps to explain why taste and smell are so useful for encoding the random, yet no less powerful, memories of contexts past than, say, vision or words" (89). Like Sutton, I think that food is not a random part that completely recalls a memory to life. Bread's synesthetic qualities, when culturally elaborated as they are in Omar's bakery, are a significant feature in everyday expressions and displays. Thus it can seem, as William Chapman (1979, 46) writes, that "the past is at its best when it takes us to places that counsel and instruct, that show us who we are by showing us where we have been, that remind us of our connections to *what happened here.*" This conception of the past helps explain why certain localities can evoke entire worlds of meaning. These sorts of evocations occur when men talk in the bakery about life.

The argument here is for an ethnography of the sensory experience of places as a way of interpreting food's evocative powers. This argument can be extended and broadened to suggest parallels between how food is remembered and how the past is remembered more generally as *a time for men*: an examination of men as men as well as a sentimental and intellectual connection between what some men know about the world and what they hope to achieve for themselves and their loved ones.

OUT OF THE PAST

The talk of men in the bakery was highly nostalgic, and accounts of the bakery tended to be told in the imperfect tense: "We used to . . ." This nostalgia was for simpler times in Egypt when bread was seen as more natural, that is, less processed, and more commonly shared. Such accounts were stimulated by questions about a particular food or "the times we live in." These narratives seemed to take on lives of their own as one person built on the memories of another and suggested other examples of the shift from earlier times to the present. But the synthesis of bakery dialogues indicated the separation of past from present, the fact that the past was indeed past. For Mustafa Hashim, rice with *samna baladi* evoked his pride as a man, eating what men should eat, nostalgia, and the comfort of repeated family habits. Recipes, cooking, and meals were filled with satisfaction and captured delightful moments for him and his family.

We use memory to establish who we are, a form of testimony about ourselves that we occasionally put on display. Memory can be a dramatic device of urgent import that shapes how we deal with our past and present and what we think of as our future. Our memories exert a powerful influence on our subjectivity and our behavior. They also structure the form and expression of our manifestations in life as we live it.

Memory is a storehouse that brings to mind personal and relational constructions. *Samna baladi* concerns historical repertoires that constitute both collective and private memories. I distinguish between individual and collective memory. Only individuals remember, but societies organize these memories or other representations of the past into collective scenarios of themselves. The function of collective memory is to establish individual memories of the past. What is important in those collective scenarios is how we establish some kind of relationship to and identification with them.

We seem to think of a meal as fleeting. When consumed, its concrete essence does not remain. Yet Karen Blixen, who wrote under the nom de plume Isak Dinesen, reminds us that when Babette cooked the titular meal of the novel, she re-created a historical epoch (Dinesen [1958] 2001). Her elaborate preparations for the feast and her cooking filled the house with "warmth and sweet smell." She was not simply a cook; she had been the world-famous chef of the Café Anglais in Paris. Men had dueled over her, for she alone knew how to turn a dinner into a love affair in which body and spirit were one. Although the poor villagers did not know it, they were dining upon the entire sum of Babette's lottery prize. They were eating the most lavish and costly feast the once world-famous Babette had ever prepared at the Café Anglais. As they ate, the little group found itself full of an unprecedented intoxication of mind, heart, and body. Usually silent at meals, on this night they somehow found their tongues loosened and their hearts melted. Blixen tells us what we already know: that the consumption of food is connected socially to all else in life and the mind, including previous and future acts of consumption. Meals are carriers of memories. For Mustafa, Omar, and his friends at the bakery in Cairo, cooking, baking, and telling stories are three vibrant forms of pleasure and pain of these "agent[s] of memory" (Diner 2001, 8). Fragments of history and memories of food reflect their lives, the worlds with which they are connected, and the balance between loss and healing.

Constructions of memory are also about the ways in which processes of remembering depend on the possibilities of "disremembering." This is not to say that forgetting is the loss of information; rather, disremembering is an incorporated aspect of remembering or sorting out the past. Or as Elizabeth Tonkin (1995, 9) puts it, "People talk of the 'past' so as to distinguish 'now' from a different 'then,'" and she is not categorical about whether it is memory or history. Her main objective is to understand individual stories as social interactions. A fruitful outcome of her approach is that she listens carefully to the person telling the story. She makes a note of the location and includes temporality: "The representations of pastness that these interconnections involve include the occasion, when teller and listener intersect at a point in time and space, as well as the times recounted" (9). For Tonkin, narration exists only within, and can be articulated only through, social relationships.

A more image-oriented approach than Tonkin's can be seen in the work of Roland Barthes (1981), who wrote that photography records what we cannot record existentially. When engaging with a photograph, one can never deny that what it reveals was actually there. Regarding the way that meals relate to individual pasts, we can argue, following Barthes's lead, that food, like photography, does not necessarily say what is no longer, but only and for certain what has been. I am not concerned with the objective truth that food signifies, but with the subjective truth of private "workings of memory," individuals' "postmemory" (Hirsch 1997), and the experiences and veneration of visions from a significant moment in time. One obvious constraint on the use of recollections is that stories are based on remembering and forgetting. They create and invent traditions; when emotions are invoked, the truth is not altogether clear or coherent. Human memory is irregular and fragile, and people feel obligated to edit the disorder of human life (Lowenthal 1985). The use of food in narratives of men being in the world is rather awkward despite the significance of the accounts, because they are image stories. Dialogues and remarks regarding food are carelessly conveyed, yet it is just this method that contains the spirit and gives vitality to foods as significant stimuli to memory. Motivated by Ricoeur's (1984) observations, my approach to personal narratives and performances of experiences is twofold: they are fundamental as instructions in human experiences through time, and they provide our only means of allowing us to hear individual, evocative memories of being a man.

Recollections try out the myriad ways in which memory, personal biography, and critical historical moments are manifested in subjective dispositions to the past and in the imagination of possible futures. Memory is also an emotional agent of precarious lives. That is, memories are not merely stocked-up images trotted out of the brain on appropriate occasions, but are formed as dynamic negotiations between past and present. To quote Paul Antze and Michael Lambek (1996, xxix), "Identity is not composed of a fixed set of memories but lies in the dialectical, ceaseless activity of remembering and forgetting, assimilating and discarding."

For Halbwachs (1980), collective memory, the intersection of memory and society, was the central issue. He argues against considering memory as an exclusively individual faculty. To remember is to be attached to collective orientations that allow memories to be synchronized in time and space. Memories are not only obtained through society, but also recounted, recognized, and located socially. Cherished meals convey visions of both dispersing from and belonging to a point of reference; to remember, we need to recognize and understand particular relations and to know and, to a certain extent, share references. Nora likewise distinguishes between history and memory; for him, a site of memory is "any significant entity, whether material or non-material in nature, which by dint of human will or the work of time has become a symbolic element of the memorial heritage of any community" (Nora and Kritzman 1996, xvii). Consequently, in my examples of Egyptian men eating food from favorite street vendors, these food stalls become concrete sites "where memory crystallizes" (xvii).

Nora and Halbwachs make slightly different comparisons. In looking at the difference between artificial history and true memory, Nora maintains that memory, by its nature, is living, while history is not only constructed but also reconstructed. Nora is clearer than Halbwachs regarding memory as an aspect of being in the world—that is, everyday memory is created between individuals and sentimental recollections and attachments.

For my interlocutors, passions for particular cuisines, along with recollections of dishes and ways of cooking them, included personal and collective moments. They were absorbed into each man's everyday life. Accounts were told from men's perspectives in a way that offers a rare insight into the neglected area of Arab men's moments of sentimentality. The accounts reveal something significant about the attachments of men, particularly how men, and not only women, are zealous carriers and keepers of everyday domestic knowledge and practices. We are in the realms of nurturing masculinities. Like Pagnol and Blixen, Mustafa, Omar, and his friends tell us what we already know: that the consumption of food is connected socially to all else in life. For men in Cairo, food stories are agents of sweet memories, pleasures, worries, and notions of gender. Food stories reflect their lives, the worlds with which they are connected, and ideas about what men do when they are men.

CHAPTER 4

WITH PLEASURE AND HEALTH

AFTER A VERY LONG ABSENCE, I am still recognized. Shop-keepers call my name, and I can still find my way and re-member the shortcuts in Bulaq. In June 1980, Farouk Man-sour, a true *ibn al-balad*, had said that it was time I visit his *hara* (lane). I was spending the summer in Cairo writing a paper on healing and popular religion in Egypt. Farouk took me, along with his daughter, who was about six years old at the time, to visit his mother's apartment. She received me with open arms. Since then, I have visited Bulaq regularly and have been fortunate to take part in many aspects of its people's everyday joys and worries. Young couples who mar-ried during my first visit in 1980 now have grandchildren go-ing to school. Girls and boys who were attending primary school have jobs and families. The babies I carried in my arms have gone to university or technical colleges and are now engaged or married. When I ask, usually teasingly, they still reply, also teasingly, that they, the people of Bulaq, are *awlad al-balad*.

The noun *balad* means "community" in the sense of vil-lage, town, or country; in colloquial Egyptian Arabic, it means downtown too. The adjectival form, *baladi*, means "local." It is used to describe residents of certain popular inner-city districts. *Baladi* is the opposite of *afrangi*, which refers to a modern way of life. *Baladi* is used by those who regard themselves as *ibn al-balad* (plural, *awlad al-balad*), a

sociocultural category that constitutes the basis of their authentic Egyptian male identity. Among some general ideas
about what my interlocutors said in defining themselves as
awlad al-balad, one in particular stands out: *ibn al-balad* is a
"ragel"—a man—a congenial man. This quality is expressed
in words that describe a man who has the ability to create a
lighthearted, warm atmosphere. Which quarter of Cairo the
men are from and what they eat are significant parts of who
they are and what they wish others to think of them. Cer-
tainly, these observations are not novel; food scholars, most
famously Jean Anthelme Brillat-Savarin ([1825] 2011), have
explained how food is part of identity and how humans define their identities in part through gastronomic practices.
The connections created by nurturing and provisioning were
significant ingredients when my interlocutors explained how
sharing food should connect family and friends in atmospheres of conviviality and conversation.

In this chapter, I examine how food is part of men's display of their sense of congeniality. Their interactions are recounted in the order of their occurrence because I wish to
demonstrate the points at which congeniality involves aspects of lightheartedness. My approach is directed toward
understanding congenial activity through the structure of its
social setting and through the social relationships of partici-
pants. In Bulaq, as in Egypt in general, ties to family, friends,
and neighbors are important and enduring. I am not deny-
ing that Egyptians, like all people, have family battles. The
global financial crisis that began in 2008 and the 2011 revolution have exposed growing tensions and conflicts within
Egyptian households. The ties that I write about reflect men's
"conjugal ethos," the values and traditions of food that my
Bulaqi interlocutors want to uphold as a way of life. Indeed,
these are standards and ideals for the people they want to be
and the lives they wish to lead. Like all ideals, they often remain only ideals. Nonetheless, they are important because
they convey something of men's ideal notions, particularly of
how they wish to act in the world.

In essence, food is at the core of men's sense of conjugality, and food must be eaten "with pleasure and health" (*bil hana wal shifa*). The potency of food as a powerful marker of identity and relationships and as a source of pleasure and satisfaction was understood by my interlocutors, since congenial settings reproduced their reputation as *awlad al-balad*. Besides their insistence on the need for congeniality around food, what was notable among them was the extent to which the simplest dish of street food, like *koshari* (a mixture of pasta, rice, and lentils) served on a tin plate and eaten with a spoon that is cleaned in the same water after each customer, could be understood through the notion of a man being an *ibn al-balad*.

Expressions such as "with pleasure and health" are sensory responses to food that offer fascinating entry points for understanding food as a site for a male ethos. In the now-classic *The Interpretation of Cultures*, Clifford Geertz (1973, 127) writes, "A people's ethos is the tone, character, and quality of their life, its moral and aesthetic style and mood; it is the underlying attitude toward themselves and their world that life reflects." I use Geertz's interpretation of ethos as "tone" and "aesthetic style and mood" when I argue that food has to be placed within the context of men's sensory articulations of congeniality. Hence, food is a site where men can be men through their presentations, actions, roles, and responsibilities. My interlocutors' understanding of themselves as authentic Egyptian men, based on a shared consensus of values and norms, can serve as a foundation for a cultural understanding of Egyptian men. Food resonates with attitudes and emotions relating to men's understandings of self and others and their underlying interactions. The ethos is then about the aspiration and fulfillment that food provides as part of a struggle to overcome economic constraints in defense of culture and tradition, religion, and hope.

A MAN KNOWS HIMSELF

Right from the start, Farouk Mansour, who is in his midsixties now, explained: "*Ibn al-balad* means you are from inside Cairo. A man from here [Bulaq] is a real *ibn al-balad*, because he knows himself. He loves being Egyptian, has vitality, and is very gallant, convivial, good-humored, brave. He is good and respectable, he doesn't play games, he chitchats but keeps his word, and he puts his fate in God's hands." An *ibn al-balad* likes to think that his blood is especially lighter than that of other Egyptian men. To have light blood is to be quick witted and fun. Farouk talked about traditional moral obligations, which include the protection of one's home and neighborhood, obedience to parents, and goodness to the needy.

In July 2013, I went to Bulaq to wish my interlocutors a blessed Ramadan and to tell them that I had almost finished writing the book. I also wanted to ask Farouk and his friends how I should connect *awlad al-balad* and food. They repeated what they had told me many years ago: generosity, gallantry, and a quick wit. Then one of the men wanted to tell me "one more story to take with [me]." Hamza Badawi, Farouk's nephew, was in his late thirties. I have known him since he was a teenager. He began:

> When I married, my wife could not cook. She was the only girl on five boys in her family. Her parents spoiled her very much. When I asked for her hand, her father told me, Zeinab is not just any girl—she is a princess. Her mother told me that Zeinab is very particular about what she likes or does not like. That she is not used to housework. Her father had insisted that Zeinab should have an education and a clean job as a teacher or in a government office. My family warned me that she would be demanding and that I would work myself to death. But all I could think of was Zeinab the princess. So I married a princess who does not like oranges, potatoes, rabbit, or the smell of onions. As God is my witness, I have kept my promise to her parents. I am better at cooking than she, but I have taught her how to cook rice and vegetables. She does not like to fry, so I do that, or her mother comes to help. Now we have two children, who will probably be as spoiled as Zeinab.

FIGURE 11. Friendly bantering about Zeinab's shopping while visiting relatives with Hamza and Zeinab Badawi in Old Cairo, 2012.

Hamza sighed and settled back in his chair. Farouk and the other men had nodded knowingly and teased along the way, saying, "*Ya batal, ya prince*" (you hero, you prince).

TIDBITS FOLLOW TIDBITS

A few days after my conversation with Hamza, I visited Zeinab, also in her midthirties, who was at her parent's home to make sweets for Ramadan and the upcoming feast. Her father, Abu Zeinab, a strict-looking man in his early sixties who owned, according to Zeinab, "the best oriental pastry and sweet shop in the whole of Egypt," joined in our conversation about ingredients, recipes, and techniques of Ramadan desserts. The conversation quickly turned to how festive foods break the routine of everyday life. I took this opportunity to ask Abu Zeinab whether there were special festive foods an *ibn al-balad* must have. He replied:

> A true *ibn al-balad* works hard to obtain the food required for each festive occasion. We want our family to be happy and not be ashamed, . . . [which would happen if] there is not enough to go around to our neighbors and visitors. It is important that there is enough to make everyone happy and spread a jovial atmosphere. You know we Egyptians like to laugh and crack a joke. Look outside the window—this is our place.

Outside were stalls of sweets decorated with arabesque-embroidered cloth and festooned with lights. Every lane we passed on our way to Zeinab's home had either stalls selling dough to bake at home or freshly fried tarts filled with raisins and doused in thick cinnamon syrup. Men trickled strings of dough onto sizzling griddles, arranging them in mounds of shredded wheat. The streets were full of the delightful fragrance of hot sugary syrup and spices. Round, small, very rich, and very sugary cookies, *kahk*, and *ataïf*, which are small filled pancakes dipped in syrup, are among the dearly loved delicacies for this particular feast.

My field notes from earlier that year (February 5) contain similar observations:

> Festivals always seem to be in progress in some quarter of Cairo. People I have interviewed these past months love merrymaking. Nearly every week brings some excitement to historic Cairo—some saint to be honored, memory to be cherished, or rite to be performed. Egyptians like to enjoy themselves. They think the blood in their veins is lighter than any other people. Interlocutors are complaining about the Brotherhood wanting to forbid festivities they regard as inventions (non-Islamic). They see them as doom and gloom, which goes against the Egyptian sense for laughter, merry-

making and for children to dress in lively colors. Fathers want to take their children to street vendors and buy dazzlingly colored violet, red, and green syrups, syrupy soaked pastries "in all the colors of happiness," Farouk said.

So that readers might, if they wish, try to make some of these sweets themselves, here is Abu Zeinab's recipe for *ataïf* for a family of five:

About two cups plain flour
About two cups of warm water
About a spoon of fresh yeast
A good teaspoon of sugar
You dissolve the yeast with one teaspoon sugar and a little warm water. Leave it until it begins to bubble. Have the flour in a bowl and add the yeast mixture and work it well into the flour. Add the remaining warm water. Work the batter until it's smooth. Put the bowl aside in a warm place. You will see that it becomes bubbly and a little elastic.
Half a kilo of white sugar
Less than half a liter of water
A few drops of lime
A teaspoon of orange blossom water
Heat it together until you get your syrup.
On the side, you have your chopped pistachio or almonds with sugar.
Fry small, round, fattish pancakes on only one side. Put the filling of nuts on the pancake, and fold the edges together. Deep fry in very hot oil, drain, and dip in syrup. Can be served hot or cold. Enjoy with pleasure and health.

Each feast or rite of passage has its special breads, pastas, sweets, and meat casseroles. Food invitations and food gifts were social calibrators among my interlocutors, each being *ibn al-balad* and concerned that feasts be flamboyant displays of their generosity and enthusiasm. The *kahk* and *ataïf*, Abu Zeinab explained, "must be there at home for visitors."

Dereliction of hospitality was unthinkable: "If you have a poor neighbor, you go with your *kahk* or *ataïf* or something else festive. A man like me cannot accept that my neighbor is not happy. You know we Egyptians are very generous people. Something sweet and tea for people passing by creates a nice festive atmosphere." Abu Zeinab, like all my interlocutors, was very particular about sweets and fruits. Men who could afford to bought seasonal fruits and the sugar required for homemade sweets, all of which are associated particularly with feelings of well-being, warmth, and welcome, of being able to provide, of crowds of family and friends making merry, and of showering everyone with hospitality.

In Bulaq, food stories recounted by my interlocutors implicitly and explicitly contrasted their behavior with that of what they see as stingy and ungallant men who try to be modern. These stories were directed at identity making and at the fulfillment and satisfaction that food provides; as the popular Egyptian saying goes, "Tidbits follow tidbits." Conviviality is created through food. The power of shared dishes and meals forges ties and creates atmospheres or ambiences that are part of the process of building and reaffirming these men's reputations as *ibn al-balad*.

Perhaps one of the earliest anthropological studies of *ibn al-balad* is by Sawsan el-Messiri (1978). Drawing on eighteenth- and nineteenth-century Arabic sources and a series of interviews, she provides an analysis of the social groups from which *awlad al-balad* emerge. This indigenous urban population of Cairo is a unique social group characterized by specific vocational orientations—merchants, craftsmen, artisans, tradesmen, and skilled and unskilled laborers. *Awlad al-balad* live in popular inner-city historic quarters of Cairo, neighborhoods that influence how their residents know the world and act in it. Most interesting is el-Messiri's description of the everyday features of Egyptian men's lives in popular quarters and the importance of personal qualities, such as being bighearted, gallant, savvy, and quick-witted, as well as having a casual attitude toward money. An *ibn al-*

balad has a strong sense of the imperative to do what is right. Hence, wealth does not matter as much as the ability to meet his obligations as a man (el-Messiri 1978).

In a manner not unlike el-Messiri, Evelyn Early (1993) provides a vibrant narration of *baladi* culture in Bulaq. Early's definition of *baladi*, which mingles Bulaqi women's perceptions and practices, has been extrapolated on the basis of its opposition to *afrangi* (53). The term *"baladi"* defines a lifestyle in Early's perspective, which also includes her female interlocutors' personal lives, dreams, fantasies, and disenchantments. Much of the same could be said about my interlocutors' social relationships, though perhaps more diffusely. To a certain degree, many of the men's relationships had, from their point of view, a highly compassionate component—there were sharply defined obligations and expectations based on gender and family—but these were not prescriptions concerning how men must interact so much as socially recognized standards employed discursively as arguments about obligations to their relationships. That is, relationships were always constituted from an array of potentialities that became actualized through their performance—which overwhelmingly involves, in one way or another, food.

Indeed, that food creates social relationships is a longstanding observation in anthropology that goes back to Mauss ([1967] 2002) and was revisited in a wide range of contexts. What was notable among my interlocutors was not only how their food relationships endured through generosity and wit, but also how much their lifestyles and identities were understood explicitly through food. These relationships defined a lifestyle, including specific, culturally perceived activities that determined gender roles, such as relating to a spouse, raising children, and socializing. Food was at the core of the men's relationships and obligation to be responsible; as an aphorism they often repeated to me put it, "We have eaten bread and salt together, so I must ask after your well-being."

To be an *ibn al-balad* was to weave together the elements of masculine social decorum needed to navigate life as an Egyptian man. His identity centers on internalized self-images (such as being a savvy and generous man) and on externalized everyday practices (such as food provision). Being an *ibn al-balad* defines a lifestyle that is described by my interlocutors as *asil* (authentic; old stock).[1] Farha Ghannam (2002) recalls *Kalam Rigalla* (Men's talk), an Egyptian film about a native of Bulaq who is elected to parliament and finds himself in a world of sinister political maneuverings:

> He is pressured to take a bribe, his son becomes a thief, and his greedy wife helps the son in selling the stolen products. The wife in particular has stopped listening to him, tries to imitate upper-class women, and pressures him to acquire more money. He finds the only solution to his problems is to go back with his son to his "authentic" neighborhood, go back to his old work, and eat the food that he used to eat before. (79)

Finally, he takes his whole family back to their old ways of "authentic" Egyptian life; life is good again, and he regains his savvy, upright, and jovial self.

It was while I was interviewing butchers about the shopping habits of Egyptian men that my attention was first drawn to the notion that men's sense of decorum and joviality was an aspect of the idioms of food. In Bulaq, Abdel Rahman Badawi, a butcher, told me simply that "a butcher has to be an *ibn al-balad*." I knew that for ordinary Egyptians, meat at a meal signals affluence or festivity, but I did not see the link between being a butcher and being an *ibn al-balad*. El-Messiri (1978) recounts how the idea of a butcher as an *ibn al-balad* was "so firmly fixed in the minds of the interviewees that, when asked why a butcher should be an *ibn al-balad*,

---

1. Not coincidentally, perhaps, the word *asil* has entered English as a term for describing Thoroughbred horses, all of which trace their bloodlines back to Egypt and Arabia.

they could give no explanation other than simply assert-
ing that 'he must be an *ibn al-balad!*'" I told Abdel Rahman
that I needed more than just "he must be *ibn al-balad*," and
added that I had met a few women who were butchers, which
showed that not all butchers were men. Yes, he said, he knew
of women who were butchers:

> They are butchers because there is no man to take care of
> them. A woman does this job because life circumstances
> force her to do it. It is not right. This is not a job for a
> woman. A butcher is like the owner of the coffee shop.
> I don't know why, but we stay in our place (*hetta*), even if we
> move away. Of course, some butchers and owners of coffee
> shops get really rich. But also they stay in their quarter. Even
> if I am a couple of times a week in my other shop in a chic
> part of town, I still have to be here in my original shop. This
> shop and this place have given me a good life. I cannot leave.
> You see, I am a totally real *ibn al-balad*.

CALVES' FEET AND A LITTLE FLIRT

Mutton and lamb are the most widely used and favored meats
in Cairo; they are also present at festive and ceremonial repasts. Said fifty-two-year-old Abdel Rahman Badawi:

> The correct thing is that the man buys the meat. A man
> works and struggles to buy a nice cut of meat. My customers,
> they come here. Sometimes they can't buy. But you know,
> we Egyptians, we like to haggle, in a good-humored way.
> The Egyptian man likes to be happy. He doesn't like gloom.
> So he knows that if he goes home with a piece of meat at
> least once or twice a month, his wife will leave him in
> peace. Otherwise, she will complain to this one and that
> one. A man wants his peace of mind. He brings home meat
> every now and then and all is calm.

Abdel Rahman was reflecting on my question about his male
customers who buy meat. I watched as he carved a front

shank of mutton, sliced the meat horizontally, removed bits in the sections, and then handed them over to his younger brother and assistant. This was in 2012, after the revolution, and Egypt was in a deep financial crisis. Food prices and unemployment had been rising since the previous year. Abdel Rahman, who had inherited the butcher shop from his father, commented on the drop in meat consumption: "I don't think they suddenly decided to eat vegetables to lose weight. If it continues like this, people will eat salad for the Eid."

Not much had changed since I first visited the shop, in the 1980s. Then, his father, Hag Badawi, was still working. The place still had the feel of a traditional butcher shop, its hard stone and sawdust-coated floors soaking up blood and catching bits of fat to prevent slipping. The original wooden doors with large metal handles still divided the shop from the cool room. Hag Badawi had eight children, five girls and three boys. "My father fed my mother very well," Abdel Rahman said laughingly. His sisters and brothers all took turns working in the shop. Both brothers worked as his assistants, and his sisters as the cashier. Most butcher shops did not have a separate cashier, but Abdel Rahman liked to use some *afrangi* ways in his business. As I continued to watch him, he gestured to the meat he was cutting and asked me again about my butcher in Norway. I had told him that I live close to a local family-run butcher shop established in 1904. Aside from the growing number of halal butcher shops owned by immigrants, I think "mine" is the only traditional butcher shop in the capital, Oslo. Abdel Rahman really liked the idea that people come from across the city to buy their meat and sausages from "my" butcher. "It's just like here then," he said. "The *usta* [expert] must be a *khawaga* [foreigner], *ibn al-balad*. I want a picture of him. You have to take a picture of me also." The crowd that had gathered around us burst into laughter.

To stand inside the butcher shop and look out is to be in the middle of local cultural, social, industrial, political, and economic affairs. I watched the people that passed by out-

FIGURE 12. A butcher at work, 2013.

side; they stopped to exchange pleasantries with Abdel Rahman and his brothers and sisters. It had been a long time
since anyone paid attention to my presence; instead, I was included in the latest news. Since 2011, conversations have always turned to politics. Everyone was democratic, and everyone had an opinion on the Muslim Brotherhood, the military,
Mubarak, Sadat, Nasser, and King Farouk. What was best for
Egypt? Conversations always ended with a joke.

Abdel Rahman's butcher shop in Bulaq was on a lane with
stone curbs. This neighborhood, located on the northeast-
ern bank of the Nile, was founded in the thirteenth century.
Historically, it was known for its textile market, mechanics,
welders, carpentries, charities, and clinics. Early (1993) offers
an excellent ethnography of Bulaq and the people, especially
the women, who live in its crumbling buildings. Next door to
the butcher shop is a repair shop with scraps of iron scattered
everywhere, then a coffee shop and a baker. On the other side
of the lane are a chickpea vendor, a popular restaurant, and a

barbershop. There are goats grazing on garbage piles, people selling ducks and rabbits, a young boy carrying a tray with tea to the welder. An endless parade of scooters steers between carts loaded with bricks and iron, massive cauliflowers, tomatoes, and lettuce. Clothes flap from ropes on sticks angled from balconies; people looking out of windows greet some, insult others, or just watch. Everyone interacts in some way or other. Private life mingles with public life.

On a later visit to Abdel Rahman, I asked him more questions about his trade. I wanted to go back to my question about men and meat, but in addition I had taken a special interest in the vanishing trade of artisanal butcher shops. He answered, "This trade demands a lot of emotional and physical strength. Raw meat and blood is not for women. So an *ibn al-balad* takes the meat home to you ladies so that you can prepare us the beautiful dishes with your sweet hands." When I teased him about whether it was also an *ibn al-balad* quality to sweet-talk every woman, he replied, "It's our nature. We like a little flirt from here and there." Then he became serious again:

> But I want to tell you this for your book: I love my trade. I am proud of it. And I love Bulaq, the smell of Bulaq, and the good people of Bulaq. I feel for the other men who don't have my possibilities. As a man, I know that every man wants to walk into his house with head held high because he knows everyone is happy. His children and wife have food and clothes and a home. For a man to bring meat is important, especially for the festivities.

As always, shoppers stopped by, but this time the vegetable vendor and the grocer stood with us. They were interested in our conversation; it touched a common interest and a passionate chord.

The conversation turned to the price of food and meat. Abdel Rahman defended his prices and explained that his meat was top quality. The other men assured him that they knew he was a good man. Still, "It is not easy for a man with a family to feed," one of the shoppers said. Abdel Rahman's sister and I sat close together and listened. There was a break in the stories. The atmosphere was gloomy. The grocer, Bakir Radwan, whom I have known since the 1980s and who was then sixty-two years old, had been standing by the entrance for some time. He said loudly to nobody in particular, "Pray to the Prophet," and people mumbled back the appropriate response. Bakir turned to me and said imploringly, "Let me tell you the story of Goha," the antihero of Egyptian folklore, a simpleton whose reasoning and actions take any proposition to the limits of absurdity. As the story began, smiles spread around the room:

> One day, Goha goes to the market with his son. Goha is going to buy a sheep. He sees one he likes and begins to stroke it and weigh its tail with hands. His son asks, "Baba, what are you doing?" Goha tells his son, "I am investigating if this sheep is good enough to buy." He decides the sheep is good and buys it. Then a few days later, when Goha was going to sit down for his supper, his son tells him, "Baba, baba, our neighbor was here in the morning. He is going to buy mama."

Roars of laughter filled the room.

I took the opportunity to ask about their favorite meat dishes, which included grilled meats, stuffed lamb, and calves' feet. "Kawareh [calves' feet] is what I love the best. I insist that my wife bone the kawareh before serving them. It is a beautiful dish," said one shopper, who liked to be called by his pet name, Moody. Smiling all over his face, Moody, who had just turned forty years old, told us that he was moving to a larger apartment. We all congratulated him, but he was ambivalent. The new place was in one of the new suburbs of Cairo. I wanted to know more about his move and why he was worried. He agreed to meet me the following week.

A couple of days later, I went back to the butcher shop.

FIGURE 13. Bakir Radwan posing in front of his nephew's store, 2012.

Abdel Rahman was working unhurriedly. "Enough of this gloom," he said:

> Now it is my turn to tell you about my favorite dish. It is the one I love the most. But I did not want to tell you in front of all the people. It is personal. And now, after the revolution, many of the men you saw here last time struggle to bring food home. My favorite dish is the first meal *el madam* [his wife] made for me: meat with okra. Here, I will phone her so she can give you the recipe.

He dried his hands, found his mobile telephone, walked to the far side of the shop, and talked to his wife. "Here": he handed me his phone. A young woman's voice at the other end told me how happy she was to share her recipe with me. "You have to let me know if your husbands like it," she teased. Then she asked me whether I had a pen and paper. While I looked for my notebook, I heard Abdel Rahman and his brothers in the background enthusiastically chatting about their favorite dishes.

"Now sweetie," Laila begins:

> We must have our *samna baladi*; you have your meat from Abdel Rahman or the butcher where you live abroad. We must have our *bamia* [okra], onions, garlic, tomatoes in tins. And of course salt and pepper. Fry the meat and okra in *samna baladi*. Now, cook onions and garlic in *samna* until they are golden. Then you take the meat that you have cut in cubes and brown it in the *samna*. Pay attention; this meal takes a lot of *samna*. Now, you have already washed the okra well and cut off the stems. You add your okra to the meat and onions and fry gently over a low fire. Now you can put a couple of tins of tomato. Let it all cook for about three hours. The meat must be very tender, falling apart. Make sure to always increase the water. Some like to add a squeeze of lemon. Abdel Rahman does not.

She wished me the best of luck and told me not to hesitate to call again for other recipes, which I have since done many times.

THE WAY HE SCOOPS HIS BEANS

A week later, I met up with Moody in Farouk's coffee shop. Moody replied laconically to my questions about how he thought his life would be different in his new apartment. When the conversation lagged, he got up, went across the street, and came back with a tin plate of *ful* for us to share. We tore small pieces of bread and folded them into cat's ears to scoop up the *ful*. Moody became more talkative; he admitted that he would miss his street, the people, the noise, dirt, smells, food, and lightness of blood:

I am moving to a place where people put on their suits and go to work. They spend money on showy stuff; we don't do that here. I spend on food for my family. I will move to a place with a supermarket. Everyone goes around pushing the cart and buying one tomato, one squash, two onions, half a piece of white cheese, five breads in a plastic bag, and one chicken full of hormones. [When] I go to shop, I come home with two *baladi* chickens [free-range chickens], two kilos of tomatoes, twenty breads from the oven. And I will insist that my wife use all the food for one meal.

I wanted to ask him one more question. "Ask anything you want," he said, casually sipping his tea. Did he compliment his wife on her cooking? "After every meal, I tell her, 'Bless your hands, *ya* Maha,'" he replied.

We went back to talking about his move out of Bulaq. While he was looking forward to more space and fresher air for the children, he knew he would never get used to being too long away from Bulaq and its disorder. "I like to move between all the food places and greet all my friends. Everybody knows me here. When we went to check out our new apartment I told Maha, *el madam*, look at the people around us. They are the ones that buy one cucumber and one chicken." He became very quiet and asked, "What are you saying about us in your book?" I was not prepared for this question, and like many other researchers when caught unawares, I mumbled something fleeting and abstract. Then it struck me as a unique opportunity to ask a key question: "What do you want me to say about you?" He smiled and took out of his pocket what looked like a folded, heavy, whitish, coarse cotton napkin, the edges stitched with thick white thread. In it is a piece of bread with white cheese, globally commercialized as feta. Moody's mother was a seamstress. She sewed all her family's clothes, napkins, bed linens, curtains, and even towels from the textiles that her customers left for her to do with as she pleased. Throughout Moody's childhood, his mother would get up before "the neighbor's rooster" to prepare breakfast and a couple of midday sandwiches for each member of the family. She would fold one of her napkins around each sandwich. Now that he is married, Moody's wife prepares a sandwich that he takes wrapped in his cotton napkin. He continued:

> Yes, now you are a good researcher. I want you to say that this [he looks down at the napkin] is just a napkin and humble, but it makes me happy. This piece of bread and cheese is about the tastiest food I can think of, and it gives me peace in my soul. And this [he point out at the lane in front of us] is, for me and all us from here, not dirty and slummy. This [again pointing around the lane] is the real and traditional Cairo, with all its disorder, commotion, and liveliness. Here life is tough, but it has a taste. It is full of spirit. We are the tough guys. Nobody messes with us, but we protect the good. This place makes us who we are. We have light blood, [we are] awake, and our eyes are wide open, we see everything.

Moody's move out of Bulaq was voluntary, unlike, for example, the forced relocations of five thousand families from Bulaq between 1979 and 1981. Ghannam's (2002) powerful ethnography is about how residents of Bulaq were moved to new public-sector housing complexes in al-Zawiya al-Hamra. She shows how new, modern apartments were designed to enhance family privacy, individuality, and hygiene. While the residents welcomed the amenities, they also strove to re-create spaces of their own within the constraints of soulless buildings that denied Bulaqi autonomy, cooperation, and support.

I met with Moody after his move, and he was happy about the space and the fresh air, which "was probably very good for the children." But he felt that the new place had "no soul or ambience," and he missed the narrow lanes, zigzagging between peddlers and scooters. "Bulaq opens up my appetite," he reflected. Did he keep to his old ways in his new flat?

The Egyptian man in general, and an *ibn al-balad* in particular, loves his family and home. It is true we go out to work and then we like to spend time with our friends joking and playing backgammon in the coffee shop. We are men. But we go home at the end of the day. For us, the family meal is sacred—sitting around the *tawla* [low table] or, for the younger generations, a high table, eating our food with our hands or a spoon. We don't use fork and knife and stuff like that. Then a man feels like a man with family and loved ones. We are together and close, and we share the same casserole.

Moody had seen me draw scenes from my fieldwork many times. He pointed across the lane at his uncle's housewares store and said, "Like this casserole." I saw it. He added, "I think you should draw the things I describe. It will help you when you write your book. And it will give an artistic touch." I made a couple of quick sketches on a brown paper bag while he talked: "Since my children were very small, I showed them [how] to fold the piece of bread into the ear of a cat and eat *nono nono* from the edge. We will continue this in our new place. I feel very uneasy eating with fork and knife. It becomes too much commotion around the meal."

Moody was not the only one who talked about the discomfort of sitting at a table arranged with "glasses, plates, spoons, forks, and knives on top of a tablecloth." Although most of my interlocutors ate their meals while sitting around high tables, nonetheless the tables were small and the atmosphere was one of informality. As Moody put it, "Not only because we don't have space for much, but also because I like to be close to my children when we eat. We all sit and reach out from the same casserole or plate. I can see that everyone is eating."

BIGHEARTED, LIGHT BLOODED

Farouk Mansour the coffeehouse owner, Hamza Badawi the taxi driver, Bakir Radwan the grocer, and Abdel Rahman Badawi the butcher were among my interlocutors from Bulaq. Their lifestyles were difficult to judge in absolute terms, given that the socioeconomic situation in Bulaq, as in several other historic neighborhoods in Cairo, includes differentiations based on education and economic activity and that the men may interact differently as individuals within a wider national sociopolitical framework.

There is a return to gentleness in this chapter, as in the book, which shows how unquiet moments and daily unpredictability can be combined with local, intensely ethnographic considerations of profound human sentiments and relationships. In *Être et avoir*, Gabriel Marcel ([1951] 1989) calls this "enthusiasm for living." By applying this approach methodologically to my fieldwork in other countries in the Middle East, and more recently in Brazil, I want to raise questions about how aspirations, anticipation, sensory experiences, aesthetics, and humor—all types of senses—can be empirically investigated and theoretically conceptualized. Providing, preparing, and eating food involves such an immediacy of sensory experiences that anthropology should be able interpret how men create and re-create their own ways of doing and of being men. This perspective relates to the reorientation of anthropology that I mentioned in the introduction and that brings out ordinary human feelings and actions that deconstruct stereotypes about, for example, bighearted and light-blooded Egyptian men.

Writing about a butcher's favorite meat dish or how a man wants to eat his food or see his table set concerns the construction of meaning and life stylization (Moore 2011). I argue that variations in the elaborations of sensory expressions and experiences, whether of taste or humor, are invested with sensations that give them meaning because they are shaped by my interlocutors' personal stories. Hence, I pick up my argument from the introduction on how men's food activities enact societal and individual experiences of being in the world. The language of food used by my interlocutors was about flavor, of course, but also about their sense of being and their relationships to others.

Consider, for example, David Howes's (2003) critique of

Nadia Seremetakis's emphasis on how the sensory experiences of certain foods gather people around very specific cultural contexts. For Howes, Seremetakis does not consider "how sensory phenomena may function as social symbols apart from, or in association with, specific individual or collective memories" (44). I think that it is most useful to understand our interlocutors' sensory facets, to understand how they fit together.

As Judith Farquhar (2002, 57) asserts with regard to strictures imposed by structuralist anthropology:

> The tangible qualities of food, like those of perfume, are not so readily forgotten. Nor are they easily disciplined within the confines of a "logic." The analytic power and tidiness of structuralist analysis in the Lévi-Straussian manner gratifies me as an anthropologist even as it annoys the eater in me, for explanatory power about signification seems to be gained at the expense of the poetry—the flavors and pleasures—inherent in everyday reality. The structuralist analyst works through the concrete to reach the logical, leaving the charms of the mundane experience far behind.

The question then, for me, is not whether men's recountings are tidy or messy, but how they are both. That is, I am intrigued by the ways my interlocutors' varying sensibilities for flavors, pleasantries, and jokes intersect the conviviality surrounding food and say something more about the many different facets of men's sensory lives. I am not saying that men in this chapter, or indeed in this book, go around being "sensory" about food all the time. Rather, it is I, after listening to their associations with food, who proposed that aesthetics and lighthearted comments made up the sensory repertoire in their male identity making and that these sensibilities led to associations about how they express and experience the world. I see both aesthetics and humor as part of the sensory and sensibility ties mooring Egyptian men to their social worlds.

FIGURE 14. Conviviality and congeniality in the narrow lanes of Cairo.

Indeed, the origins of the study of aesthetics lie in the philosophical study of art. In its regular use, the concept of aesthetics connotes high culture and class-based processes of discrimination and distinction (Bourdieu 1977). It is most commonly used to refer to what is visually and auditorily pleasing, although gustatory and kinesthietic perception may also be thought of as "aesthetic" (Feagin and Maynard 1997). Normative judgments and standards of artistic beauty—described as "serious sensuous perception"—provide a central perspective in the art-located study of aesthetics and often generate the notion that beauty carries universal validity (Cootes and Shelton 1992, 8). Art historians such as Svetlana Alpers (1983) and Michael Baxandall (1972) draw our attention from art objects to the culture of perception. They demand an explicit understanding of how other cultures "see" the world. Aesthetics has gained visibility in anthropological analysis as part of a move toward the senses and sensibilities that surround human life and practice. Its key concepts, anchored in representations of everyday life, are seen by many as at best difficult and at worst "luscious imaginary" (Holtzman 2009, 58). Meanwhile, at the method-ological bases, the aesthetics of food is still under construc-tion (Adapon 2008). It evokes a number of approaches that seek alternative lines of analysis in tune with non-Western ontologies.

The aesthetic experience of food, broadly conceived, forms the basis for a varied range of ordinary, everyday activities. Thus, Arnold Berleant's (2010) interpretation of aesthetics as the active engagement of human beings in and with their complete world of experience is relevant to my assertion. Ber-leant presents aesthetics as "what is perceived by the senses" (4). Aesthetics, therefore, is not confined to rigid, predefined patterns, but is actively constructed, cultivated, and, most of all, sensed through the ongoing processes of being in the world (Gell 1998). This embedded approach to aesthetics is not unlike the ways that Angela Hobart and Bruce Kapferer (2007, 5) define aesthetics as "being primary" and as prac-tice—"what ties art (as all other human endeavors) to life." Hence, regarding Abdel Rahman, Bakir, and Moody, I suggest that the men and their associations are essentially an aes-thetic force; to paraphrase Hobart and Kapferer, these men's food associations anchor their endeavors "in which life is shaped and comes to discover its direction and meaning" (5).

SENSE OF HUMOR

Humor is a category of Egyptian life that has not featured strongly in anthropological analysis, at least not in relation to men. The somewhat depressing approach of most such analysis is perhaps not surprising, given the lack of social or gender equality and the doctrinaire lines common to reli-gion. In Middle Eastern studies in recent years, the most sus-tained attempts to elaborate on humor, as a descriptive and an analytical category, have come in studies of the perform-ing arts and media. This work emphasizes the character of wit, creativity, and humor as well as the fact that a sense of humor gives social reality a historical character and inserts it into long-term explorations of people and society.

In episodes like the ones recounted above, a question related to the notion of the irrepressible predisposition of Egyptians to claim lightness of blood could open up new opportunities to understand how men feel about their obligations. The interplay between discourse, activity, and social order has become the dynamic point of interest. This interplay, as shown in light-humored moments, is about freedom from form and, at the same time, about a particular shared social structure where a joke can be told. There is a broad range of classic anthropological studies on humor, laughter, and joking (Apte 1985; Douglas 1968; Handelman and Kapferer 1972; Radcliffe-Brown 1940), but most of them are limited to humor that occurs in situations of relative social stability. There remains a need to discuss the place of humor in times of social crisis. I propose that in times of acute uncertainty, such as periods of political or social disorder, jokes call social norms into question.

But humor also imparts to those who partake of it a sense of orderliness and normalcy that may otherwise be lacking. In other words, when social relations are severely disturbed, making jokes not only compels us to think beyond existing social norms but also, in doing so, implicitly suggests that there are limits to life's inconsistencies.

My interlocutors enjoyed trivial moments when conversations went in all sorts of directions; since they were with men living under harsh economic conditions, it was perhaps not surprising that they indulged in this type of humor. I am attempting to look closely at the trivia of everyday jokes and relationships. Ordinary happenings and conversations, such as men standing in a corner and joking and affectionately teasing each other, can easily go unnoticed in our data because they are cultural regularities about life's irregularities. But that is what makes such events significant. These underlying patterns and structures reveal themselves in trivial features of social life. The challenge is to underline the humor; jokes and light conversation bring us closer to understanding the links between social locations and human relationships. This is an opportunity to revive Mary Douglas's (1975, 149) classic theory of the joker as a community's philosopher—it can be anybody and everybody:

> The pleasure of a joke lies in a kind of economy. At all times we are expending energy in monitoring our subconscious so as to ensure that our conscious perceptions come through a filtering control. The joke, because it breaks down the control, gives the monitoring system a holiday. . . . For a moment the unconscious is allowed to bubble up without restraint, hence the sense of enjoyment and freedom.

People raise perennial issues regarding the relationship between thought and experience, and related activities reduce the dissonance between different realms of experience and ambience.

Expanding on Douglas's everyday philosophy of life, I suggest that the lighthearted episodes in my recountings are part of men's social lives and expressions of appreciation of community in its least hierarchized and differentiated aspect. Like rites, instances of humor and puns connect men to everyday life. When I carefully asked whether they joked all the time, the person who joked least said that it would be difficult for men to speak with each other without couching suffering in a joke: "Under the circumstances, it's instead of committing suicide!" Such a strong statement implies that humor keeps men at a safe distance and protects them from life's disenchantments. Their playful conversations, witty exchanges, and puns survey the system of relationships that becomes part of people's life projects and social control. In Douglas's (1975) approach, this interplay between humor activities and social order becomes the animated expression of everyday life.

CONCLUSION

PEOPLE CONSTRUCT THEIR WORLDS AROUND water, land, plants, food, housing, clothing, and relationships to other people and living beings. If we follow these basic human needs, we can piece together stories about men, women, and children that record pivotal life experiences and social patterns. Taken overall, and because it is so extraordinary, food emits as many varied messages as any other aspect of human culture. Insights into social life and relationships gained from a study of blacksmiths and from one of bond traders would differ. And so it is with food and people's accounts of it. In this book, I attempt to identify, within a group of men in Cairo, significant sets of food experiences that constitute ways of living life and provide important messages about men and their ethos. These messages operate on different levels; they present multistranded identity markers, interactions, and relationships.

Fahmi, Rafat, Ahmad, Mustafa, Abdel Rahman, Moody, Farouk, Hamza, and Bakir provided my observations about men's life experience told through the lens of food. I attempted to reveal only the men's own words that expressed food's self-fulfillment. Indeed, the exploration of food as a marker of identity and social interaction has a long history in anthropology, going back to Audrey Richards (1939), which I would argue is the best ethnography on food. My approach in this book is to show not only the wide range of relation-

FIGURE 15. Nurturing: men buying bread on their way out of Friday mosque and heading to their family lunches, 2012.

ships constituted through food, but also the extent to which provisioning and male ethos are defined and understood explicitly through the idiom of food. Ultimately, I hope that my ethnography successfully imparts the extent to which men, their identities, and their relationships are constituted through the idiom of food.

The food events recounted in this book are formulations and descriptions about notions of manhood. They are based on the premise that daily food experiences and provisionings symbolize more than gender and household domains in the Middle East reflect more than Arab identity and power systems. Rather, because food is such a potent symbol of culture and lifestyle, its associations become ethnographically rich and provide us with possibilities to develop trenchant theories about individual worlds, social order, and cultural complexity. Elaborate festive food and regular family lunches reproduce the enduring aspects of notions of manliness in Egypt; in particular, food should be seen as a medium through which manliness is displayed explicitly through caregiving. Anthropologists should freshen our theories to reveal the unending potentialities of fieldwork in enriching our insights.

Living according to the social order of things requires individuals, as Barth (1989) argues, to absorb "cultural streams." Hence, people are linked with other people through several cultural streams in their attempts to form an encompassing tradition. Food has the potential to penetrate the cultural streams that allow people to share attributes with others. My material shows how food is linked with several areas of men's daily lives, all of which generate some sort of shared understanding about what it means to be a particular sort of man. Food, then, is a core component in Egyptian manliness and men's relationships with family and friends.

A MAN WANTS A TIDBIT TO GO HOME TO

The main point of *Nurturing Masculinities* is the simple yet complex idea that food is a powerful marker of manhood, fatherhood, and family structure in contemporary Egypt. This book makes two central arguments. The first is that food creates a core social bond between men and their households and community. The second is that food serves to overturn the Muslim Arab masculinity slot, since it marks or mediates men as active and practicing nurturers. And yet in assembling these accounts, I wanted to do more than simply bring together men's lives and highlight their relationships to food. These narratives of food and masculinity challenge the view of the undomesticated Arab Muslim man. My interlocutors' lives have been compiled and textualized in this book to show that the world is messy and cannot be presented in neat compartments of men's and women's worlds.

I have coined the term "nurturing masculinities" as a conceptual trope to explicate men's life experiences and to show the importance of men in food studies. My approach is deliberately multistranded, examining different areas where food, domesticity, and men intersect with patterns of masculinities in Egypt, a country typecast as a place of callous manliness, dismal surroundings, and dejected relationships. These stories are from different men who live under particular social, cultural, and political conditions. By watching them move among their families, friends, and surroundings, I constructed what I intended to be a nuanced and accurate view of Egyptian men, and in general Middle Eastern men, and daily living. I introduce and address a range of anthropology-inspired questions intended to stimulate more food studies in Middle East scholarship. I hope that the conceptualization of nurturing masculinities contributes to the emergence of masculinity studies in the Middle East and elsewhere.

Nurturing Masculinities is an effort to bring food forward as an anthropological, scholarly, and real-life concern. What makes food such a powerful arena of masculinity in Egypt? How does food construct men's terrain of nurturing and relationships? What does it say in particular about Egyptian men? To what extent can lessons from this book be extended to studies of food, human life, and gender in other societies?

Answers to these questions must in some way center on the sensory act of eating and on related emotional caring practices. Yet there is far more to this interpretation, which is rooted mainly in how food serves as a medium for constructing the most significant relationships: the intimate, the public, and the avenues in between. Food belongs, as Andrea Wiley (2006) notes, consummately to both the material and the transcendent, and thus is one of the few arenas that remain relatively untouched by the often-fractious debates concerning its continuing value. I am not raising this point to undermine Claude Lévi-Strauss's terminology that food is "good to think," or Marvin Harris's that food is "good to eat" ([1985] 1998). Indeed, this book is about the many things food is "good for"; these strands exponentially reinforce food's potential and serve as windows onto a particular ethos. And so it is that food is a good way for men to be men.

In my accounts there emerges a certain image of the Egyptian Muslim man working hard to provide food for his family and share tidbits with his pals. In effect, food experiences allow us to contextualize and consider the ways that men and domestic life are intertwined, particularly if we focus on the ways that public food handling is reinforced by everyday responsibilities and obligations. Food is an especially appropriate topic to lead us to considerations about men's everyday lives and their experiences of well-being, since paying attention to food demands that we look more closely at how people buy, prepare, share, and eat it.

THE SALT OF LIFE

I am reminded here of *Le sel de la vie* [The salt of life], a book by the French anthropologist Françoise Héritier (2012). Héritier's book deals with small occurrences and gestures that give humans the most profound experiences of well-being and pleasure. My interlocutors, in the different field sites and topics of my research, likewise brought up, in one way or another, life aspects that gave them pleasure.

Omar Saad was among the youngest of my interviewees. He was, in his own words, "a street kid." I have known him since he was a small child selling flowers on the street corner of an upscale Cairo neighborhood. Recently, he called to tell me that thanks to a mobile phone and a motorbike, he is now able to make home deliveries. But he had something more wonderful to tell me. He had finally married his childhood sweetheart, Jasmine. I remember at the time how adorable I thought it was that Omar had found a girl with a flower's name. Jasmine's father was against the marriage, but Saad was persistent: "I did not keep quiet. I convinced him that she loves only me and that only I can make Jasmine happy and comfortable. I will bring home her favorite food." Would he bring her flowers? "Why? She is the flower," he said. Now that they are married, I wanted to know whether he remembered what he once said about always making her happy. "Of course," he answered, with an offended tone in his voice, "Aren't I *ibn balad*?" Did she cook well? I heard a sigh at the

FIGURE 16. Omar Saad with his flowers, 2011.

other end. "No. I tell you the truth. She does not know how to cook at all. Yesterday she cried and cried. But no problem. There is a really nice widow next door. She is alone, so she has offered to teach Jasmine to cook the food I like." What about the food Jasmine likes? He said with a chuckle, "Of course. I get her whatever she wants to eat. But I am a married man now, with my madam at home. I want to go home to a nice tidbit. *Ya doctora*, I am a man and this is the country of men."

IN A COUNTRY OF MEN

For men in contemporary Egypt, food is rooted in their identity as men. The combination of masculinity and food in Egypt is not reducible to an embodied form; it is complicated and difficult. With conviviality, congeniality, wit, and appetite—this is how men eat.

As a "total social fact" (Mauss [1967] 2002), food poses

questions about what it means to be human. Food, as an object, and eating, as an act, resonate with human attitudes, emotions, understandings, and feelings about the self and others. This book regards a set of foodways that one might call, in the spirit of Mary Douglas (1982), a "food sentence": food and meals that produce ideas about customs associated with meals, gendered duties in regard to food, rules of responsibility and conjugality, diet and domestic economics, and politics and religion. In this Egyptian example of a food sentence, I include food moments that lend shape and meaning to men's foodways: breadlines, food activism, and conjugality.

The relationship between food and men is often neglected in Middle East ethnographies. When I turned my attention from women speaking about food to men's long elaborations on food, I was astonished to discover an abundance of information. In my attempt to concentrate on foodways that directly affect men's lives and identities, I explored not only what these men revealed about their ideas and experiences of feeding their families, but also what we can assume about creations of masculinity and care, and therefore about transformations, in Egyptian society as a whole.

My ethnography of young members of the Muslim Brotherhood underscores that, for anthropology, faith-based food activism revives questions of piety and practice as analytical units and invites us to go beneath discourses on Islamists, veils, beards, and orthodoxy. I hope that as an ethnographic study of an Islamic outreach movement in a largely Muslim country, my contribution on Islam, men, and food encourages more research into how the rhythm of faith-based activism synchronizes with the pulse of daily life and engages with concrete contemporary concerns about men and religion—and about men and religion through food.

Food and eating are narratives of human existence. They detail our relationships with other humans and with our environments. The Norwegian archeologist and ethnographer Randi Håland (2007, 1667) puts it neatly: "Food items are not only food 'for the body,' they are also 'food for thought' about our relations to 'others' in the world of living people, and to cosmological forces." Håland tells us what we already know: food constitutes attachments at different levels and of different kinds. In theory building, food tells us something about political, economic, and cultural human values (Mintz 1985). Cooking and eating both bind and tear apart nature and culture, production and consumption, morals and economy, households and state, the personal and communal, and the body and psyche.

I seek to unravel what sates a group of Egyptian men who embrace a style of life embedded in their local communities. We have seen how men construct and repair their food experiences and how, in the process, they interpret, participate, and coexist as men do when they are being men.

An exploration into food and men is an exposition of fundamental life questions, human experiences of selves and others. Much as the anthropology of Arab men is about power and conflict, and the ethnography of food about division and cruelty, both topics are also about pleasantry, caregiving, and congeniality. Men and food establish ambience, create attachments, evoke memory, give pleasure, and sate desire.

Abu-Lughod, J. 1971. *Cairo: 1001 Years of the City Victorious*. Princeton, NJ: Princeton University Press.

Abu-Lughod, L. 1989. "Zones of Theory in the Anthropology of the Arab World." *Annual Review of Anthropology* 18:267–306.

———. 2013. *Do Muslim Women Need Saving?* Cambridge, MA: Harvard University Press.

Adapon, J. 2008. *Culinary Art and Anthropology*. Oxford: Berg.

Alpers, S. 1983. *The Art of Describing: Dutch Art in the Seventeenth Century*. Chicago: University of Chicago Press.

Altorki, S. 1999. "Patriarchy and Imperialism: Father-Son and British-Egyptian Relations in Najib Mahfuz's Trilogy." In *Intimate Selving in Arab Families: Gender, Self, and Identity*, edited by S. Joseph, 214–234. Syracuse, NY: Syracuse University Press.

Antze, P., and M. Lambek. 1996. "Introduction: Forecasting Memory." In *Tense Past: Cultural Essays in Trauma and Memory*, edited by M. Lambek and P. Antze, 11–13. New York and London: Routledge.

Appadurai, A. 2007. "Hope and Democracy." *Public Culture* 19 (1): 29–34.

Apte, M. L. 1985. *Humor and Laughter: An Anthropological Approach*. Ithaca, NY: Cornell University Press.

Bahloul, J. 1996. *The Architecture of Memory*. Cambridge: Cambridge University Press.

Bakhtin, M. M. 1981. *The Dialogic Imagination*. Translated by Caryl Emerson and Michael Holquist. Austin: University of Texas Press.

Baron, B. 2005. *Egypt as a Woman*. Berkeley: University of California Press.

Barth, F. 1989. "The Analysis of Culture in Complex Societies." *Ethos* 54 (3–4): 120–142.

———. 1993. *Balinese Worlds*. Chicago: University of Chicago Press.

———. 1994. "A Personal View of Present Tasks and Priorities in Cultural and Social Anthropology." In *Assessing Cultural Anthropology*, edited by R. Borofsky, 349–361. New York: McGraw-Hill.

Barthes, R. 1979. "Toward a Psychosociology of Contemporary Food Consumption." In *Food and Drink in History*, edited by R. Forster and O. Ranum, 166–173. Baltimore: Johns Hopkins University Press.

———. 1981. *Camera Lucida: Reflections on Photography*. Translated by R. Howard. New York: Hill and Wang.

Basso, K. 1996. *Wisdom Sits in Places: Landscape and Language among the Western Apache*. Albuquerque: University of New Mexico Press.

Baxandall, M. 1972. *Painting and Experience in Fifteenth Century Italy.* Oxford: Clarendon.

Berleant, A. 2010. *Sensibility and Sense: The Aesthetic Transformation of the Human World.* Exeter, UK: Imprint Academic.

Boddy, J. 2007. *Civilizing Women: British Crusades in Colonial Sudan.* Princeton, NJ: Princeton University Press.

Bourdieu, P. 1977. *Outline of a Theory of Practice.* Translated by Richard Nice. Cambridge: Cambridge University Press.

Bourdieu, P., et al. 1999. *The Weight of the World.* Translated by Priscilla Parkhurst Ferguson. Cambridge: Polity.

Brillat-Savarin, A. 2011 [1825]. *The Physiology of Taste: Or Meditations on Transcendental Gastronomy.* Translated by M. F. K. Fisher. New York: Vintage.

Bruner, E. M. 1986. "Introduction: Experience and Its Expressions." In *The Anthropology of Experience,* edited by V. W. Turner and E. M. Bruner, 3–30. Urbana: University of Illinois Press.

Burgat, F. 2002. *Face to Face with Political Islam.* Oxford: I. B. Tauris.

Carsten, J. 1995. "The Substance of Kinship and the Heat of the Hearth: Feeding, Personhood, and Relatedness among Malays in Pulau Langkawi." *American Ethnologist* 22 (2): 223–241.

———. 1997. *The Heat of the Hearth: The Process of Kinship in a Malay Fishing Community.* Oxford: Clarendon.

Chapman, W. 1979. *Preserving the Past.* London: Dent.

Charsley, S. R. 1992. *Wedding Cakes and Cultural History.* New York: Routledge.

Connell, R. W. 1995. *Masculinities.* Berkeley: University of California Press.

Connerton, P. 1989. *How Societies Remember.* Cambridge: Cambridge University Press.

Cootes, J., and A. Shelton. 1992. Introduction to *Anthropology, Art and Aesthetics,* edited by J. Cootes and A. Shelton, 1–11. Oxford: Clarendon.

Counihan, C. 1988. "Female Identity, Food, and Power in Contemporary Florence." *Anthropological Quarterly* 61 (2): 51–62.

———. 1999. *Anthropology of Food and Body: Gender, Meaning, and Power.* New York: Routledge.

Counihan, C., and S. Kaplan, eds. 1998. *Food and Gender: Identity and Power.* Amsterdam: Harwood Academic.

Davis, N. J., and R. V. Robinson. 2012. *Claiming Society for God: Religious Movements and Social Welfare.* Bloomington: Indiana University Press.

Delaney, C. L. 1991. *The Seed and the Soil: Gender and Cosmology in Turkish Village Society.* Berkeley: University of California Press.

Diner, H. R. 2002. *Hungering for America: Italian, Irish, and Jewish Foodways in the Age of Migration*. Cambridge, MA: Harvard University Press.

Dinesen, I. (1958) 2001. *Babette's Feast*. London: Penguin.

Douglas, M. 1966. *Purity and Danger: An Analysis of the Concepts of Pollution and Taboo*. London: Ark.

———. 1968. "The Social Control of Cognition: Some Factors in Joke Perception." *Man* 3 (3): 361–376.

———. 1974. "Deciphering a Meal." In *Myth, Symbol, and Culture*, edited by C. Geertz, 68–81. New York: Norton.

———. 1975. *Implicit Meanings*. London: Routledge.

———. 1982. *In the Active Voice*. London: Routledge.

Early, E. 1993. *Baladi Women of Cairo: Playing with an Egg and a Stone*. Cairo: American University in Cairo Press.

Farquhar, J. 2002. *Appetites: Food and Sex in Post-Socialist China*. Durham, NC: Duke University Press.

Fassin, D. 2012. *Humanitarian Reason: A Moral History of the Present*. Berkeley: University of California Press.

Feagin, S. L., and P. Maynard, eds. 1997. *Aesthetics*. Oxford: Oxford University Press.

Feeley-Harnik, G. 1994. *The Lord's Table: The Meaning of Food in Early Judaism and Christianity*. Washington, DC: Smithsonian Institution Press.

Gardiner, M. E. 2000. *Critiques of Everyday Life*. New York: Routledge.

Garro, L. C. 2000. "Remembering What One Knows and the Construction of the Past: A Comparison of Cultural Consensus Theory and Cultural Schema Theory." *Ethos* 28:701–712.

Geertz, C. 1973. *The Interpretation of Cultures*. New York: Basic Books.

Gell, A. 1998. *Art and Agency*. Oxford: Blackwell.

Ghannam, F. 2002. *Remaking the Modern: Space, Relocation, and the Politics of Identity in a Global Cairo*. Berkeley: University of California Press.

———. 2013. *Live and Die like a Man: Gender Dynamics in Urban Egypt*. Stanford, CA: Stanford University Press.

Gilroy, J. P. 1987. "Food, Cooking, and Eating in Proust's *À la Recherche du Temps Perdu*." *Twentieth Century Literature* 33 (1): 98–109.

Gilsenan, M. 1996. *Lords of the Lebanese Marches*. London: Tauris.

Goody, J. 1982. *Cooking, Cuisine and Class: A Study in Comparative Sociology*. Cambridge: Cambridge University Press.

Gottschalk, P. 2000. *Beyond Hindu and Muslim*. New York: Oxford University Press.

Greenfield, S. 2000. *The Private Life of the Brain*. London: Penguin.

Gutmann, M. C. 1997. "Trafficking in Men: The Anthropology of Masculinity." *Annual Review of Anthropology* 26:385–409.

Hafez, S. 2012. "No Longer a Bargain: Women, Masculinity, and the Egyptian Uprising." *American Ethnologist* 39 (1): 37–42.

Håland, R. 2007. "Porridge and Pot, Bread and Oven: Food Ways and Symbolism in Africa and the Near East from the Neolithic to the Present." *Cambridge Archeological Journal* 17 (2): 165–182.

Halbwachs, M. 1980. *The Collective Memory.* New York: Harper and Row.

Handelman, D., and B. Kapferer. 1972. "Forms of Joking Activity: A Comparative Approach." *American Anthropologist* 74:484–517.

Hannerz, U. 1996. *Transnational Connections.* London: Routledge.

Haraway, D. 1988. "Situated Knowledge: The Science Question in Feminism and the Privilege of Partial Perspective." *Feminist Studies* 14 (3): 575–599.

Harris, M. (1985) 1998. *Good to Eat: Riddles of Food and Culture.* Prospect Heights, IL: Waveland.

Harris, O. 1996. "The Temporalities of Tradition." In *Grasping the Changing World: Anthropological Concepts in the Postmodern Era,* edited by V. Hubinger, 1–16. London: Routledge.

Harrison, S. 2006. *Fracturing Resemblances: Identity and Mimetic Conflict in Melanesia and the West.* Oxford: Berghahn.

Héritier, F. 2012. *Le Sel de la vie* [The salt of life]. Paris: Odile Jacob.

Herzfeld, M. 1985. *The Poetics of Manhood.* Princeton, NJ: Princeton University Press.

Hirsch, M. 1997. *Family Frames: Photographs, Narratives, and Post Memory.* Cambridge, MA: Harvard University Press.

Hobart, A., and B. Kapferer. 2007. *Aesthetics in Performance: Formations of Symbolic Constructions and Experience.* Oxford: Berghahn.

Hobbes, T. (1651) 1958. *Leviathan, Parts I and II.* New York: Bobbs-Merrill.

Holtzman, J. 2009. *Uncertain Tastes: Memory, Ambivalence, and the Politics of Eating in Samburu, Northern Kenya.* Berkeley: University of California Press.

Hoodfar, H. 1997. *Between Marriage and the Market.* Berkeley: University of California Press.

Hopkins, Nicholas S. 2003. "Introduction: The New Arab Family." In *The New Arab Family,* edited by Nicholas Hopkins, 1–4. Cairo: American University in Cairo Press.

Howes, D. 2003. *Sensual Relations: Engaging the Senses in Culture and Social Theory.* Ann Arbor: University of Michigan Press.

Inhorn, M. 2004. "Middle Eastern Masculinities in the Age of New Reproductive Technologies: Male Infertility and Stigma in Egypt and Lebanon." *Medical Anthropology Quarterly* 18 (2): 162–182.

————. 2012. *The New Arab Man: Emergent Masculinities, Technologies, and Islam in the Middle East*. Princeton, NJ: Princeton University Press.

Jackson, M. 2011. *Life Within Limits: Well-being in a World of Want*. Durham, NC: Duke University Press.

Jansen, W. 1997. "Gender Identity and the Rituals of Food in a Jordanian Community." *Food Foodways* 7 (2): 87–117.

Joseph, S. 1983. "Brother/Sister Relationships: Connectivity, Love, and Power in the Reproduction of Patriarchy in Lebanon." *American Ethnologist* 21 (1): 50–73.

————. 1993. "Connectivity and Patriarchy among Urban Working-Class Arab Families in Lebanon." *Ethos* 21:452–484.

————. 1999. *Intimate Selving in Arab Families*. Syracuse, NY: Syracuse University Press.

Kahn, M. 1986. *Always Hungry, Never Greedy: Food and the Expression of Gender in a Melanesian Society*. Cambridge: Cambridge University Press.

Kanafani, A. 1983. *Aesthetics and Ritual in the United Arab Emirates: The Anthropology of Food and Personal Adornment among Arabian Women*. Beirut: American University of Beirut Press.

Kandiyoti, D. 1996. *Gendering the Middle East*. Syracuse, NY: Syracuse University Press.

Khouri-Dagher, N. 1996. "The State, Urban Household, and Management of Daily Life: Food and Social Order in Cairo." In *Development, Change, and Gender in Cairo: A View from the Household*, edited by D. Singerman and H. Hoodfar, 110–133. Bloomington: Indiana University Press.

Kilshaw, S. 2009. *Impotent Warriors: Perspectives on Gulf War Syndrome, Vulnerability, and Masculinity*. New York: Berghahn.

Kirshenblatt-Gimblett, B. 1999. "Playing to the Senses: Food as a Performance Medium." *Performance Research* 4 (1): 1–30.

Kleinman, A. 2009. "The Art of Medicine: Caregiving; The Odyssey of Becoming More Human." *Lancet* 373 (9660): 292–293.

————. 2012. "The Art of Medicine: Caregiving as Moral Experience." *Lancet* 380 (9853): 1550–1551.

Kondo, D. 1990. *Crafting Selves: Power, Gender, and Discourses of Identity in a Japanese Workplace*. Chicago: University of Chicago Press.

Korsmeyer, C. 2005. *The Taste Culture Reader: Experiencing Food and Drink*. Oxford: Berg.

Kugelmass, J. 1990. "Green Bagels: An Essay on Food, Nostalgia, and the Carnivalesque." *YIVO Annual* 19:57–80.

Lévi-Strauss, C. 1966. "The Culinary Triangle." *Partisan Review* 33: 586–595.

Lia, B. 1998. *The Society of the Muslim Brothers in Egypt: The Rise of an Islamic Mass Movement, 1928–1942*. Beirut: Ithaca Press.

Lowenthal, D. 1985. *The Past Is a Foreign Country*. Cambridge: Cambridge University Press.

Marcel, G. (1951) 1989. *Being and Having*. Translated by K. Farrer. Boston: Beacon.

Mauss, M. 2002 [1967]. *The Gift*. London: Routledge.

Mennell, S., A. Murcott, and A. H. van Otterloo. 1992. *The Sociology of Food: Eating, Diet and Culture*. London: Sage.

Messiri, S. el-. 1978. *Ibn al-Balad: A Concept of Egyptian Identity*. Leiden: Brill.

Mintz, S. 1985. *Sweetness and Power: The Place of Sugar in Modern History*. New York: Viking Penguin.

———. 1996. *Tasting Food, Tasting Freedom: Excursions into Eating, Culture, and the Past*. Boston: Beacon.

Mintz, S., and C. M. Du Bois. 2002. "The Anthropology of Food and Eating." *Annual Review of Anthropology* 31:99–119.

Moore, H. L. 2011. *Still Life: Hope, Desires and Satisfactions*. Cambridge: Polity.

Munson, Z. 2001. "Islamic Mobilization: Social Movement Theory and the Egyptian Muslim Brotherhood." *Sociological Quarterly* 42 (4): 487–540.

Naguib, N. 1996. *Med Kall til Ledelse* [Men of commitment]. Oslo: Universitetsforlaget.

———. 2009. "Tastes and Fragrances from the Old World: Memoirs by Egyptian Jewish Women." *Studies in Ethnicity and Nationalism* 9 (1): 122–127.

———. 2010. "For the Love of God: Care-giving in the Middle East." *Social Sciences and Missions* 23 (1): 124–145.

Nelson, C. 1974. "Public and Private Politics: Women in the Middle Eastern World." *American Ethnologist* 1 (3): 551–563.

Nora, P., ed. 1984. *Les Lieux de mémoire: La République*. Paris: Gallimard.

———, ed. 1986. *Les Lieux de mémoire: La Nation*. Paris: Gallimard.

———. 1989. "Between Memory and History: Les Lieux de mémoire." *Representations* 26:7–25.

———, ed. 1992. *Les Lieux de mémoire: Les Frances*. Paris: Gallimard.

Nora, P., and L. D. Kritzman, eds. 1996. *Realms of Memory: The Construction of the French Past*. Vol. 1, *Conflicts and Divisions*. Translated by Arthur Goldhammer. New York: Columbia University Press.

Pagnol, M. 1989 [1957]. *Le Château de ma mère* [My Mother's Castle]. Paris: Editions de Fallois.

Pink, S. 2012. *Situating Everyday Practices and Places*. London: Sage.

Rabo, A. 2006. "Affective, Parochial or Innovative? Aleppo Traders on the Margin of Global Capitalism." *Revue des mondes musulmans et de la Méditerranée* 115–116:43–58.

Radcliffe-Brown, A. R. 1940. "On Joking Relationships." *Africa* 13: 195–210.

Richards, A. 1939. *Land, Labour, and Diet in Northern Rhodesia*. Oxford: Oxford University Press.

Ricoeur, P. 1984. *Time and Narrative*. Vol. 1. Translated by Kathleen McLaughlin and David Pellauer. Chicago: University of Chicago Press.

Roden C. 1999. *The Book of Jewish Food*. London: Penguin.

Rosaldo, M. 1980. *Knowledge and Passion: Ilongot Notions of Self and Social Life*. Cambridge: Cambridge University Press.

Rosaldo, R. 1993. *Culture and Truth: The Remaking of Social Analysis*. London: Routledge.

Sahlins, M. 1999. "Two or Three Things I Know about Culture." *Journal of the Royal Anthropological Institute* 5:399–422.

Scheper-Hughes, N. 1992. *Death without Weeping: The Violence of Everyday Life in Brazil*. Berkeley: University of California Press.

Shehata, S. 2012. *Shop Floor Culture and Politics in Egypt*. Albany: State University of New York Press.

Singerman, D. 1997. *Avenues of Participation*. Cairo: American University in Cairo Press.

———. 2004. "The Networked World of Islamist Social Movements." In *Islamic Activism: A Social Movement Theory Approach*, edited by Q. Wiktorowicz, 143–163. Bloomington: Indiana University Press.

Stoller, P. 1989. *The Taste of Ethnographic Things*. Philadelphia: University of Pennsylvania Press.

———. 1997. *Sensuous Scholarship*. Philadelphia: University of Pennsylvania Press.

Sutton, D. E. 1998. *Memories Cast in Stone*. Oxford: Berg.

———. 2001. *Remembrance of Repasts: An Anthropology of Food and Memory*. Oxford: Berg.

———. 2008. "A Tale of Easter Ovens: Food and Collective Memory." *Social Research* 75 (1): 157–180.

Tadros, M. 2012. *The Muslim Brotherhood in Contemporary Egypt: Democracy Redefined or Confined?* Abingdon, UK: Routledge.

Tannahill, R. 1988. *Food in History*. New York: Random House.

Thompson, E. 2000. *Colonial Citizens: Republican Rights, Paternal Privilege, and Gender in French Syria and Lebanon*. New York: Columbia University Press.

Thompson, E. P. 1991. "The Moral Economy Reviewed." In *Customs in Common*, edited by E. P. Thompson, 259–351. London: Merlin.

Tonkin, E. 1995. *Narrating Our Pasts*. Cambridge: Cambridge University Press.

Turner, V. 1969. *The Ritual Process: Structure and Anti-Structure*. Piscataway, NJ: Aldine Transaction.

Vaughan, M. 1987. *The Story of an African Famine: Gender and Famine in Twentieth-Century Malawi*. London: Cambridge University Press.

Weismantel, M. J. 1988. *Food, Gender, and Poverty in the Ecuadorian Andes*. Philadelphia: University of Pennsylvania Press.

Wickham, C. R. 2004. "Interests, Ideas, and Islamist Outreach in Egypt." In *Islamic Activism: A Social Movement Theory Approach*, edited by Q. Wiktorowicz, 231–247. Bloomington: Indiana University Press.

Wiley, A. 2006. "The Breakdown of Holism and the Curious Fate of Food Studies in Anthropology." *Anthropology News* 47 (1): 9, 12.

Wilk, R. 1999. "'Real Belizean Food': Building Local Identity in the Transnational Caribbean." *American Anthropologist* 101 (2): 244–255.

Zahid, M. 2012. *The Muslim Brotherhood and Egypt's Succession Crisis: The Politics of Liberalisation and Reform in the Middle East*. London: Tauris.

Zubaida, S., and R. Tapper. 2000. *A Taste of Thyme: Culinary Cultures of the Middle East*. New York: Taurus Parke.

Italic page numbers indicate photos.